Secrets of the Softer Side of Selling

Second Edition

Donald S. Crawford

Lois Carter Crawford

Secrets of the Softer Side of Selling
Second Edition
by Donald S. Crawford and Lois Carter Crawford

ISBN-10: 0-9742511-4-3
ISBN-13: 978-0-9742511-4-1
(Paperback Edition)

Published October 2017

Author photos courtesy of Swartz Photography, Harrisonburg, Virginia.
Cover photo courtesy of iStockPhotos.
Book design by Emily June Street at Luminous Creatures Press.

Published by:
Marketing Idea Shop, LLC
Harrisonburg, Virginia 22802 / USA
Email: lois@softersideofselling.com

Websites:
www.marketingideashop.com
www.softersideofselling.com

CONTENTS

CHAPTER ONE

Introduction

Secrets of the Softer Side of Selling, Second Edition focuses on how everyone can use their "soft skills," or relationship and communication skills, to improve their sales performance.

We wrote the first edition of ***Secrets of the Softer Side of Selling*** with a special focus on women to help them take advantage of their natural communication skills to become better salespeople. Because women often have good communication and organization skills, we think they can be excellent salespeople.

Although gender can play a role in selling, the art of personal selling is not gender-specific. It is relationship-driven. Remember, even if you are not a professional salesperson, everybody sells. Developing better sales skills could be just the ticket you need to move up the corporate ladder or become the entrepreneur you always hoped you would be.

This book is written for you, the professional salesperson. You qualify if you are one of these:

- A small business owner
- An entrepreneur
- A solopreneur
- An independent sales rep
- A salesperson working for a business
- An employee who has an occasional need to sell as part of a sales team
- A manager of people who have a full-time or part-time selling roles

How to Use *Secrets of the Softer Side of Selling, Second Edition*

This book is organized linearly, one chapter following another, because that's the way books have to be. But in a real, live, selling situation, all of what is in this book can happen in any order and may occur simultaneously.

The skills build on each other and can also be learned and used independently. Once you have studied all the skills and techniques and put them to into practice, it's likely you'll be a fabulous salesperson. So, don't panic. It may look overwhelming now, but read on. You can do this.

Discover Your Process

The art of successful personal selling is a process, and every great salesperson has one. Although they all differ slightly based on personality, experience and industry, each effective salesperson has developed what works for them. We will guide you in the process we use and help you identify and develop what works for you.

Your process may be well developed and successful, in which case you earn an income in the top 4% of your industry. If so, then use this book to help you learn to train and mentor other salespeople in your industry.

If you are barely scraping by and often wonder where the rent money will come from, take heart; we've all been there at one time or another. When you put in the effort, things will change.

As you read this book, give each technique a fair trial; then keep what works for you. Customize the techniques to your own style. Don't simply mimic what you see here. Instead, take these new ideas and put them into practice in your own way to make them yours.

The words we use or the cadence of our speech in a sales example might be awkward for you. You can either practice the words we give you until you are comfortable delivering them, or use your own words to convey the same meaning. Only rarely are the specific words needed. Generally, it's only the concept that is important.

Learn and Improve

If you're not in the top 4% of your profession, you need to change what you're doing.

Keep what's working and fix what's not.

In general, people resist change. It's easier to do what we've always done. And—you know the rest—you'll continue to have the same success (or lack of it). But if you want better results, it's time to do something different, isn't it?

So it's a choice. You can choose to stay the same or you can choose to make changes in your attitude, knowledge and activities to propel yourself to super salesperson status.

It's time to commit yourself to achieving your goals by applying yourself without distraction to the things you know (or you will soon know) you need to do.

What do You Need to Win?

The most successful salespeople have two traits: drive and ambition. "Drive" is an urge to attain a goal; "ambition" is a desire to achieve.

Do you have these traits?

You don't need to be highly educated or the brightest salesperson on the planet to become the best. If you're willing to try new ideas, learn from your experiences, and commit to being the best in your profession, you'll be successful.

What You Should Do

To get the most out of this book, here's what we want you to do:

- **Take your time.** Don't simply read; take the time to stop and think. If we ask you a question, ponder, consider, and decide on your answer. Don't skip ahead to find out what we think.
- **Do the exercises.** Don't skip them; do the work! You'll get more out of this book if you reflect upon your results and put effort into making changes. You'll really learn this material and remember it if you actually think and do!
- **Read the chapters more than once, perhaps aloud.** Repetition is a key to remembering what you read. If you read it out loud, you'll also hear it,

so you'll be learning in more than one way, which will make a big difference in how much you remember.

- **Try the techniques in your business.** If you start using these techniques, you're sure to improve your sales. But if you don't try them, you'll never know how they might work, will you?
- **Record the results.** Remember to keep track of your successes. Each success will help you stay motivated. And over time, you'll begin to see how far you've come. It's likely you will recognize some patterns in your successes, too.
- **Let us know how you're doing.** If you let us know your successes, we'll celebrate with you so you'll be even more motivated. Besides, we'll get to feel good because we helped you improve, and it's fun to spread happiness, isn't it? Even if a technique doesn't work for you, we want to know. Your feedback is essential and we may be able to help you tweak what you are doing to improve your sales. Contact us at: lois@softersideofselling.com

Let's Get Started

The first thing we want you to do is complete an honest, personal assessment. What are your strengths and weaknesses? Write them down.

Then ask your family, friends and business associates to add to the lists. Listen, evaluate their responses, and decide for yourself what should be on your inventory.

Everyone has strengths and weaknesses, and with a little training, you can turn some of your weaknesses into strengths. So get busy and list all your positive attributes along with the ones you believe need improving. Remember to keep in mind what the people you polled previously told you about yourself. You will find a Personal Inventory Form at the end of this chapter.

As you read through ***Secrets of the Softer Side of Selling,*** keep in mind your perceived strengths and weaknesses, focusing on techniques to improve the needed skills. After you finish the book, take the personal inventory again to see if you think anything has changed. And then go back through the sections for the skills that you think you need to improve.

No matter how experienced you are at selling—whether (or not) you like selling—***Secrets of the Softer Side of Selling, Second Edition*** will give you tips, techniques and advice to help you become one of the top performers in your profession.

PERSONAL INVENTORY FORM

Strengths:

- ________________
- ________________
- ________________
- ________________
- ________________

Weaknesses:

- ________________
- ________________
- ________________
- ________________
- ________________

CHAPTER TWO

Gender Differences

We all know men and women are different. Soft skills, or relationship skills, are generally thought to be skills that women easily master.

But everyone has some of each of the qualities we consider male or female, including soft skills. You know that, even if you've never read a scientific research study to prove it.

Admit it, the reality is that generalizations are "generally" true. Consider these:

Men	Women
• Competitive	• Collaborative
• Stoic	• Nurturing
• Linear	• Fluid
• Speak with few words	• Talkative
• Measured	• Emotional
• Physically stronger	• Physically weaker

The selling process, however, is the same whether men, women, or a mixed team is selling and whether the customer is male, female or a team with both genders. On the other hand, based on our experience, we think the techniques and finesse of building the relationship and "getting into the buyer's mind" is somewhat different when one gender is selling to the other.

More importantly, everyone is an individual and your sales success depends on how you can solve the "pain" your prospect has (more on this in Chapter 10).

In Chapter 9 we will discuss some personality differences that may influence how you determine the best approach to each customer or prospect. What we offer in this book is a proven process to help you sell to anyone. How do we know it works? We've been doing it for years.

At the end of each chapter, we will give you some ways to **Challenge Yourself** to help you understand and become comfortable with the concepts presented.

Challenge Yourself

1. List all the ways you believe men and women are different.

2. For each difference, write down how it affects your communication with each gender in decision-making situations.

CHAPTER THREE

Being a Great Salesperson

Are you a terrific salesperson? Let's start with a simpler question: "Do you sell?"

And the answer to the second question for everyone, of course, is: "Yes." People "sell" every day. We sell our ideas to our families, our products to our customers, and our services to our employers or clients. Whether you know it or not, you are in your own business—even if you work at a Fortune 500 company or are in a specialty field where you get all your work from one small group of existing clients—you are in the sales business. You are in the business of you.

Whether you are new to selling or an experienced salesperson, the first step is to take a look at your current situation. Who are you and who you want to become?

Take an Inventory of Your Skills

In Chapter 1, you made a list of your strengths and weaknesses. This is an important precursor to developing an inventory of your skills.

A skills inventory will help you decide who you are and where you're going. List everything you do well and then list the skills you think you need to improve. Work to improve your weaker skills while believing your skills will become stronger.

Remember, however, that what you think becomes your reality. Think: "I can improve and become the best."

Challenge Yourself

1. Use the short Sales Skills Inventory Quiz on the next page to help you discover if you are suited to be a salesperson.

2. Then focus on improving all of your skills.

SALES SKILLS INVENTORY QUIZ

Rank yourself from 1 to 10 (with 10 being the best and 1 being the worst) on the following statements.

___ I am a good problem solver.

___ I keep my goals in mind and work toward them every day.

___ If someone says "No" to me, I never take it personally.

___ I keep a list of what I need to do and I cross the items off as I accomplish them.

___ I know how many sales I made last month/week/year.

___ I am a self-starter.

___ I successfully accomplish what I set out to do.

___ I am an optimistic person.

___ I am able to handle most stresses well.

___ I am motivated to win.

___ I like to meet new people.

___ I'm comfortable shaking someone's hand when we meet.

___ I can introduce myself without stumbling over my words.

___ When I ask people to do things, they generally comply.

___ People tell me they admire me.

___ I am organized and can keep myself on task.

___ I am reliable; when I say I will do something, I do it.

___ I am persistent; it takes a lot to make me give up.

___ I am intuitive and easily understand others.

___ I am a good listener.

___ I am honest and ethical.

___ I am happy.

___ I love helping others.

___ Talking to people is easy for me.

___ I am outgoing and cheerful.

How did you rank?

175-380: Excellent sales skills
100-174: Good sales skills
75-99: Study hard!
0-74: It might be time to look for another profession

CHAPTER FOUR

Personal Selling & the Marketing Process

Before we get into the selling process, you'll need to understand a few sales and marketing terms.

What's the difference between sales and marketing? Some companies use the terms interchangeably, which is not correct. The way we look at it, "sales" gets orders; "marketing" builds awareness.

Historically, marketing has been described as the "4 P's": product, price, promotion and place.

The product aspect is concerned with the goods or services to be sold. Here, the focus is on creating a better-than-the-competition's product to meet the need of the market or developing a new product never before conceived. Think iPhone, self-driving cars or even special phone or computer applications such as Instagram and Snapchat, that everyone now thinks they have to have.

Price is all about, well, pricing strategy. Where is the product in its lifecycle? Is it a brand new product you need to teach people how to use? Has it been on the market many years with many competitors? Is it reaching the end of its usefulness? When you price your product, you will need to decide on a price that covers costs, makes a profit and keeps the competition at bay. It also affects the way that you sell the product (we'll discuss this later).

Place deals with distribution/location. How is the product delivered to the consumer? Through electronic venues or brick-and-mortar (physical) stores? Or is it clicks-and-mortar (that is, a combination of online and physical storefronts)? Is it sold directly by the manufacturer or is there a complex distribution system to get the product to market?

Promotion is where personal selling fits into the marketing mix. It is coupled with advertising, public relations (including social media, blogs and websites), customer service, sales promotions, brand awareness, direct mail, point-of-purchase displays, trade shows and sponsorships. Depending on the business model, personal selling may or may not be the most important element.

When Don goes online to order a pair of shorts from LL Bean, there is no salesperson involved. But when he buys a house or a car, you bet he's going to rely on the expertise the salesperson brings. Lois may research high-priced items online, but she goes to the salesperson to finalize her decisions.

In most business-to-business (B2B) situations—that is, businesses selling to other businesses—involving complex problem solving, a professional salesperson is invaluable. The need for a salesperson is obvious when a company is building a new factory, buying new manufacturing equipment, or looking for new raw materials.

But how about if a company sells ear plugs or paper notebooks? These items cost pennies each and the expense of getting them to the user often exceeds the cost of the item.

Salespeople can become wealthy when they help their prospects recognize the high cost of shipping is negligible compared to the potential problems caused by not having these products.

The sales and marketing relationship is often tense. Sales personnel depend on the rest of the marketing mix strategy to support their personal selling efforts with leads, collateral material, competitive pricing and products satisfying a need.

The salesperson is the first to see changes in the marketplace and their role is to bring information back to the rest of the marketing team. The salesperson represents two entities, and doing a good job with both is often like walking on a tightrope. To the customer, they represent the company. To the company, they represent the views of the customer.

Salespeople understand the customer and the problems their company can solve. Their input into developing advertising and promotion activities and materials often determines the success or failure of a campaign.

Successful salespeople build relationships with the marketing department. Sales without marketing support would be like the human hand without an opposable thumb. It would work well for swatting but couldn't do fine needlework.

Challenge Yourself

1. How important is personal, face-to-face or over-the-phone selling to closing deals for your products or services?

2. What support does the marketing department give the sales team?

3. In your business, how open are the channels of communication between marketing and sales?

4. In your company, who drives product development—the sales team or the research and development department?

5. Do the sales and marketing departments in your business speak with a single voice to the customer? If not, how can you affect change to make the value proposition or unique selling proposition message congruent?

6. Describe the distribution channel(s) used to move your company's product or service to the customer. Where do you fit in?

CHAPTER FIVE

Choosing What to Sell

In this chapter we will explain tangible and intangible products and focus on two broad sales markets, business-to-business (B2B) or business-to-consumer sales (B2C). Nonprofit organizations and government agencies are not the focus of this book, but in general, they are both subsets of B2B selling. Finally, we will discuss the different types of sales: one-time purchases, recurring sales, new buy, straight rebuy, and modified rebuy. By the time you finish this chapter, we trust you will be able to choose the best sales path for yourself.

Tangible vs. Intangible Products

Tangible products are things you can see, touch, taste, hear or smell—that is, physical items: cars, homes, vacuum cleaners, groceries, musical instruments, gravel, lumber, tools, office supplies, farm animals, perfume, etc.

On the other hand, intangibles don't exist until you buy them. You can't take them for a test drive. They are promises that a service will be performed, for example, life insurance, marketing services, massage, cleaning services, theater performances, dental work, home staging, or any other kind of service. If you're in the intangible sales business, we suggest you read ***Selling the Invisible*** by Harry Beckwith and ***Influence, the Psychology of Persuasion*** by Robert Cialdini.

Salespeople generally find they prefer selling either tangibles or intangibles. Of course, there's a component of each in everything we sell, but for the most part, we gravitate to one or the other. Which are you most comfortable with?

Consumers or Businesses

Another aspect that influences what you choose to sell is whether you are more comfortable selling to consumers or selling to businesses. The basic process for making a sale is the same, but the way the buyer decides, the motivation, and the size of the sale differ. There are also products both businesses and consumers buy—as you see if you walk into an office supplies store and observe who's shopping there.

Basically, you are either persuading a customer to part with his money in exchange for something of value (B2C sales) or you are convincing an employee or owner of a business to invest in your solution (B2B sales). For us, getting businesses to part with their money is a whole lot easier than selling to consumers. What's your preference?

Types of Sales

B2C and B2B markets provide different types of selling opportunities: one-time, recurring, new-buy, straight-rebuy or modified-rebuy purchases. Each is described below.

One-time purchases are large investments that happen infrequently. On the B2C side, purchasing a home, a car, a new furnace or a sailboat only happens once or if it is done multiple times, there is generally a long interval between acquisitions.

For the B2B salesperson, one-time purchase examples are:

- Machine tools
- A corporate jet
- A new factory
- Another company
- Naming rights for a new sports stadium

Salespeople who work in industries where the one-time purchase is the prevalent mode need to move from one deal to another. They must constantly search for new customers. There's a protracted selling cycle for major purchases; it generally takes the buyer a long time to make a decision.

That doesn't mean relationship selling is tossed aside. The salesperson needs to be engaged throughout the selling cycle. Building a reputation as the go-to person in the industry will bring prospects for future sales. Doing a good job on the current sale wins referrals to others who need your services.

New-buys are situations where the prospect is purchasing something they have never bought before. Think about a guy buying his first car or a new retailer looking to build a store.

The role of the salesperson is critical here. Most new-buy prospects have only a simple knowledge of what they need and perhaps can only explain what outcome they want, not how they want to achieve it. By asking the right questions and listening to the responses, the professional salesperson can guide the prospect through the sales process. In this case your ability to demonstrate experience and expertise in solving similar problems is important.

Recurring purchases happen regularly, again and again. In the B2B world they may be automatic sales, untouched by human hands, where computers note stock levels and signal for a delivery. For consumers it's things like buying toothpaste or a monthly subscription to cable television.

If you are the vendor of choice, your role is to make sure the customer has a moment of magic—one that impresses and surprises the customer—with each purchase. If you are on the outside looking in (that is, not the current vendor), you may need to wait in the wings for the customer to have a moment of misery (major disappointment) with their current vendor.

Other good times to approach a company that is making recurring purchases are when personnel change, when the prospect has a new product introduction, or when the capacity of the current vendor can't keep up with their demand. If you can come in with an amazing solution, you'll likely be able to pick up the business.

If you are the current vendor, the more tightly you can get your customer's business systems integrated with yours, the more difficult it will be for a competitor to take away the business. Coordination at all levels of business, from corporate management to shipping and receiving folks, is important. In fact, new ideas for partnering with customers to improve performance and reduce costs often come from all levels of the company as a result of day-to-day activities.

Straight rebuys are similar to recurring purchases except they are single events where the same product is purchased as needed, not on a regular schedule. Purchasing a new winter coat doesn't happen every year (at least not in our household). A company buying personal computers for new hires is a B2B example. For the successful salesperson, knowing the schedule of when these rebuys will occur is vital. The salesperson will need to intervene at the right moment to pitch an alternative to "the usual."

For example, when Don worked for a fire-protection company, fire extinguisher service contracts were written annually. Coming into the competitor's account at the end of the contract year was too late to make a sale. So Don trained his extinguisher sales team to check the tags on fire extinguishers while making a sales call at the companies served by their competitors. From this information they knew when the contract was up for renewal. They would then begin the sales process three months prior to the expiration date. If there was enough dissatisfaction with the current vendor, that was time enough to make a change. And as a defensive measure, Don's team would begin contacting its current customers three to four months before contracts expired to make them "bulletproof" when the competitor came calling.

Modified rebuy is when a customer wants to make a purchase similar to one made previously, but their needs have changed somewhat. A family with a new baby is ready to move up from the fun two-door sports car into one fitting the needs of a family. A business bringing out a new product line for a different market wants to purchase media advertising to reach the new target market. Being aware of the changes in your customers' companies and in their industries is important to knowing when modified rebuys are taking place. The help a salesperson provides is similar to the new purchase. Perhaps the salesperson has more knowledge of the problem and can help the customer define their need.

Great salespeople time the buying process right and engage in the process early to define the problem and offer the best solution to meet their customer's budget and goals.

Hunters vs. Gatherers

We have discussed selling to businesses or consumers and the differences between tangible or intangible products or services. Now it's time to consider your sales style. Are you a hunter or a gatherer?

You may have heard the age-old analogy that says salespeople are either hunters or gatherers. The hunter seeks new business either from entirely new companies or from within an existing customer's organization (not necessarily his current contact).

The gatherer maintains or increases a line of business with an existing customer. The gatherer is loyal and always ready to serve their existing customers even if they have to skip a new business meeting.

Salespeople generally prefer one or the other type of selling activity. Which one are you?

Don't misunderstand. You have to be good at both to build your customer base and keep it growing. But there are those who would rather have their fingernails pulled out than make a cold call on a potential prospect or look for new business at networking events. For them, maintaining a good selling relationship with a customer is a passion.

Don likes the hunt. He'd rather be out scrapping with the competition to bring in a new account. While he nurtures the mutually beneficial, long-term relationships he has developed, his passion is always with the next new conquest.

Lois, on the other hand, prefers to see what additional

services she can sell to her existing clients. She is a gatherer. It's much easier for her to sell new services to them than to find and secure new clients. Customer relationship management is more in her bailiwick.

When you're new to your sales career, you may not know where your passion lies. Try selling a variety of products to each type of market, consumers and businesses. Be a hunter and a gatherer. See which one is more personally rewarding. Then make your choice.

Challenge Yourself

1. Take a look at your own preference for selling tangibles or intangibles. Which do you prefer and why?

2. Is your comfort level with consumers or businesses? Write down why you feel comfortable with one or the other.

3. Think about the products and services you sell. Which of the traditional types of purchases (one-time, recurring, new-buy, straight-rebuy, or modified-rebuy purchases) do your best customers make?

4. What strategies can you use to win business for each type of purchasing decision?

5. Look over your prospect list. For those who make recurring, straight or modified rebuys, do you know their purchase timing? How can you create an overwhelming desire to change at a strategic time to win business away from your competitor?

6. For your best customers and prospects, are you in position to capture their next one-time or new-buy purchase? Have you built a strong relationship with the influencers and decision-makers so they

will call you when they are thinking of purchasing the kind of solutions you sell?

7. Do you enjoy the hunt for new business or would you rather gather business from existing customers? Why?

CHAPTER SIX

Characteristics of Successful Salespeople

Two characteristics you'll need if you've chosen a sales career are ego strength and ego need. Successful salespeople have healthy egos, either naturally or learned over years of experience. The stronger and more self-assured salesperson is able to handle rejection, deal with call reluctance, accept lost sales, and still keep trying.

Outstanding salespeople also have strong ego need. They're determined to achieve their dreams and quickly find ways to overcome any obstacles to success. They have can-do attitudes, employ successful behaviors and activities, and are life-long learners. Like the proverbial three-legged stool, all the legs need to be in place and equally strong. We will talk about each of these "legs" in depth below.

Leg No. 1: Attitude

First, your attitude is key to achievement and your success depends on a positive mindset. Other attitudes to strive for are being cheerful, driven, honest, fearless, outgoing, empathetic, and humble (well, a little humble, anyway). Don Miguel Ruiz in his book ***The Four Agreements*** sums up the attitude of any successful person. He says we:

- Should be impeccable with our word
- Shouldn't take anything personally
- Shouldn't make assumptions
- Should always do our best

Have integrity. Of course, being impeccable with your word means to always tell the truth, but it goes farther. The best salespeople never speak ill of their competitors. They don't gossip about one customer with another. They don't put other salespeople down. It means taking responsibility for your mistakes, and never blaming others.

It's not personal, it's business. The hardest of these agreements for Don is not taking anything personally. He hates it when he loses a sale. Overcoming the natural sting of rejection is difficult for everyone.

There are a few things you can do to ease the pain. Taking action by following up with the customer can help. One technique Don uses is to ask the customer two questions:

1. Why did you place the order with the competition?
2. What could I do differently next time to earn the business?

The customer's response is generally informative. In nearly all cases, Don finds the sale was lost for a lot of impersonal reasons. For instance, the competition did a better job of understanding needs and presenting solutions, or the pricing and delivery schedules were better.

It's also important to remember customers buy when they have a need and are ready to solve the problem. When they choose to buy, you may not be ready to sell something to them. Learn and grow from your mistakes; don't beat yourself up over them.

Learn to handle disappointment. Here's an example of what Don did. For three years Don had been pursuing business with a company building a new manufacturing plant. The project was going along well. He had secured a large order from one of the subcontractors on the project. The building was half-built and Don's company was soon to begin their part of the project. Then the announcement came. The owner had decided not to complete the project and was stopping all work immediately. An initial $300,000 order immediately disappeared.

Although disappointed, Don realized the immediate project loss wasn't too bad since it was early in the year and this amount was only a small percentage of the annual sales goal. It would be easily made up as the year progressed. However, the lifetime value of this customer, including work yet to begin with other subcontractors and service to them over the years, would be millions of dollars unless he acted quickly.

Coincidentally, when the call came in, he was in the office of one of his customers, a subcontractor who was doing work on this project. They commiserated with one another. Then, after the official notice came, Don worked the phones talking with this customer and all of the other folks he knew who had a vested interest in the project. Don steered the discussion about the current project loss toward seeking future business together, and soon they were working together on another project.

So remember, you will have failures. This one was out of Don's control. Nothing he could have done would have changed the decision by the building project's owner. Rather than wallowing in a long grieving period, he got right back to work selling. And that's what you should do, too.

Remember, you are a winner. If you don't make the sale today, it doesn't mean you are a failure. Don't take the loss personally. There will be another sales opportunity.

But you say, "I feel lousy when I lose a sale."

Yes, you may feel completely defeated for a while, but then it's time to learn from the experience and move on. Losing the sale doesn't lower your value; you are still the same terrific person you have always been. Even when you lose a sale, you are still a winner. You were born a winner and it never changes.

The point here is to separate who you are from what you do.

If you're having a bad day, walk over to the mirror, look yourself in the eye and proclaim, "I am the best salesperson in my company. I can overcome any obstacle." Doing this in public restrooms may raise a few eyebrows, but you can use it as a teaching moment and get everybody looking in the mirror and affirming in unison.

We learn valuable lessons from losses, leading us to more successes. The only people who don't fail are those who don't do. Do your daily sales activities to become successful. Celebrate your victories and learn from the undesirable outcomes.

Don't assume. We're sure you've heard the practical definition of assume: to make an ass out of (yo)u and me. As we lead you through the sales process, we'll teach you what questions to ask and how to ask them.

Lois often gets tripped up by this one. She assumes too much without confirming the details. She is so happy to solve someone's problem she sometimes forgets to ask all the appropriate follow-up questions like, "Will you sign this agreement now?" and "When should I start?"

When in doubt, ask. Nothing is more embarrassing than shipping the customer an incorrect order because you assumed you knew what he needed.

When Don managed a branch office for a safety products company, the customer service reps were the gatherers. They developed strong relationships with their counterparts at the customers' offices. A typical conversation might go like this:

Customer: "Hey, Lynn. Send me those same blue things we got last time."

Customer Service Rep (CSR): "Ok, Bill, let's look at your last order . . . wow, it's been six months since you ordered the 20 x 40 blue tarps! You sure you need the same quantity?"

Customer: "Yeah, I guess. Why do you ask?"

CSR: "Well, buying a whole pallet of tarps and tying up cash for six months doesn't seem like a good use of your money. How about having us ship you one-month's worth the last week of each month?"

Customer: "Cool idea, Lynn. Thanks for taking good care of me."

This conversation shows there was a lot going on here. For now, notice that the CSR was tuned into the customer so well she didn't have to ask what "those blue things" were. She confirmed what product he meant and offered a better cash-flow option to the customer.

If you don't know your customer well (or you don't have a good computer system to keep track of "those blue things"), you need to ask questions to make sure you understand exactly what he wants. Be sure to confirm his request before you enter the order.

Always do your best. You'll have good days and great days, and occasionally, some not-so-great days. Doing your best is relative. If you are ill, your best may not be as good as you have done in the past, but it will be your best for the current moment.

Don't spend time beating yourself up—as long has you have done your best under the circumstances. It's terrific to strive for perfection, but nobody's perfect.

Leg No. 2: Behaviors and Activities

Sales activities fall into two categories; Earl Nightingale described them as goal-achieving and stress-relieving. The basic goal-achieving activities for salespeople are setting appointments, making sales calls and doing follow-up. Stress-relieving activities are the things we do to relax and enjoy life. Sometimes you can relax and sell at the same time, however, like taking customers to supper or playing golf.

Do the work. The best attitude and the greatest knowledge are worthless if you don't take action. Successful selling consists of repeating sales activities over and over until you become the best (and then there's no reason to stop!).

Pick up the phone, and make the call. Write the follow-up email. Ask for referrals. In the next chapters we will teach you the sales process and discuss specific sales activities and tools that can help you succeed.

Leg No. 3: Life-long Learning

Salespeople who are at the top of their profession are continual learners. Outstanding salespeople are passionate about studying their profession and the industry in which they sell. They are confidently knowledgeable about their product so that they can overcome objections during the sales process.

Learn about the industry. Developing the best sales techniques is only one part of improving your knowledge. You also need to understand the industry in which your customer competes.

What are the dynamics of the industry? Where does your customer fit in? Is your customer's company:

- An innovator or a copycat? That is, the leader or a follower?
- Selling high-value products or the low-price option?
- New to the industry or the company that started it?

What problems do your customers typically have for which you can provide unique solutions? Do some research and find out. The Internet is perfect for learning about your customer, their industry, and your competitor's way of marketing.

"Become a resource and not just a salesperson," says Jane Missel, a sales consultant. "Before any sales call, I research the company and the industry by visiting their website, looking at industry social media, and reviewing their competitors. During the first meeting I ask questions about their goals and objectives, competitive advantage, anticipated changes in the next 12 to 24 months, etc. You need to know what the company is doing today, how they track return on investment and what they want from their business partners before you can offer solutions."

Attending industry trade shows can provide a wealth of information. You'll be amazed at what you can find out walking the trade show floor, talking to people and listening to the people around you.

Learn about your products. To be able to sell your company's products, you will need to know all there is to know about them. Study your company's marketing literature, talk to company management, and listen to your current customers to learn about them. What is your product's unique selling proposition? That is, what is different or better about your product compared to your competitor's product? What solutions can you provide to your customers that your competitors cannot match?

Study sales techniques. Excellent salespeople develop their sales skills in a variety of ways, such as observing seasoned salespeople doing their job, seeking and working one-on-one with a mentor, reading sales books, taking a class or workshop, and making good use of their travel time. They listen to educational and motivational podcasts, audios and CDs between appointments. They read daily (we suggest one hour per day) to improve their skills in their profession.

Stay informed. To make it to the top of the sales profession, it's important to keep up-to-date with business and world news, to be able to passionately discuss at least one topic, and to know how to keep a conversation going.

Knowledge builds confidence, and the best salespeople project a self-confident attitude as they deal with their customers. Often a confident salesperson creates a confident buyer.

Learn to ask for help. We suggest you get a mentor (or two or three). Find the best performing salespeople in your company and learn how they have become successful. Ask them to help you, or simply pay attention when you are around them. If you can't find one in your company, get one from another company or pay for training from a special mentoring program.

Learn to take care of yourself. It's important to balance work with play. Remember to schedule time to relax and take care of yourself. We get our calendars together every month and schedule playtime, which includes at least one day each weekend, and you should too.

Rest rejuvenates. Play energizes. Creativity inspires. And improving your sales skills and education brings success. Study hard. Work smart. Have fun. Repeat.

Challenge Yourself

1. Define what "professional salesperson" means to you.

2. How do you feel about the profession of selling?

3. What is your attitude toward your company, your products and your customers?

4. What can you do to improve your product and industry knowledge?

5. What passion can you discuss with your prospects and customers?

6. How do you balance your personal, family and professional obligations?

CHAPTER SEVEN

Understanding Buyer Behavior

Buyers are motivated by the functional needs of a product or service. Or they are motivated by the psychological high of getting it or the disappointment—pain—of not having it. Sometimes both. We will talk more about pain in Chapter 10.

Let's talk about Don's search for a new car.

Living in a town with very limited public transportation, a car is a necessity (functional need). And Don is of an age where mere functional considerations are not enough. It had to be a ***cool*** car (psychological need). Don's not impulsive when it comes to purchasing expensive items. Much Internet searching for the perfect car led to visits to several local car dealerships.

Then he saw it.

It was beautiful—a Porsche Boxster convertible right in the front row of the dealer's lot. With heart pumping and adrenaline rushing, Don peered at the window sticker. It was within the budget! A fast ride up the Interstate and a meandering ride back down country roads with the top down, and it was a sale.

You can't carry your grandmother's overstuffed chair in it, but hey, that's what friends with trucks are for. You can get a week's worth of groceries in it and there is enough space for luggage for a week-long vacation trip. It satisfied both the psychological need for a cool car and the functional need of transportation.

Buyers start the shopping process with recognition of a need (or want). It's your job to figure out what the need or want is.

What's the problem with the existing situation? Is the current home too small for your prospect's growing family? Is the carpet in the living room worn and soiled? Is the buyer concerned about the financial security of his family?

If the purchase would satisfy a want, what is the reason the buyer desires this product?

The next step the buyer takes is to formulate a specification, or the criteria, for the solution to their problem. What are the features and benefits of the product or service that will satisfy the need? What possible products or services will solve the buyer's problem?

You bought this book and are reading it because you need to improve your selling skills. When you do, your income will rise and you will be able to buy more of the products or services you want and need to give you the lifestyle you deserve.

You may think B2B sales are always made rationally and are functionally driven. But you would be wrong.

Consider the division manager of a manufacturing firm given the task of increasing profitability of his division by 20 percent each year. When he achieves this goal, he gets rewarded. Perhaps it's a cash bonus or maybe he's honored at a meeting of his peers for having the most improved division in the company. After several years of achievement, he gets promoted. He receives more prestige, more money.

On the other hand, if he doesn't meet the goal, he's stuck in an unhappy situation or worse...he has to explain to his wife and kids why he is home all day, every day.

As we will explain when we discuss the selling process, all sales decisions are emotional, but they are justified logically. It's important to understand not only what the buyer wants but also why he wants it and how strongly he wants it.

Who Makes the Decision?

Buying decisions are made in a variety of ways. The simplest is a single decision-maker, such as a gentleman who wishes to purchase a suit, tie and shoes, or a small business owner looking for office space. In this case, the sales professional need only be concerned with the single decision-maker.

A word of caution here. While the guy buying the new suit may look like he is all alone in this process, his wife or girlfriend may need to pass judgment on the purchase. That's the purpose of the decision-making step in the sales system. In this step, you find out who will be involved in the decision to purchase.

If there is group involvement in the decision, as there typically is in major family decisions or corporate purchases, the successful sales professional understands the roles of each of the participants. Remember, each participant has functional needs and psychological needs. In the best situation all of the participants' needs align perfectly. In the worst ones, it's like trying to negotiate with North Korea.

During the decision-maker step you have to identify the players and their roles.

The Decision Maker: This is the person with the key to the treasury. They can commit the funds. Generally, in a business, they have profit-and-loss responsibility, the most to gain from brilliant decisions and the most to lose from catastrophic mistakes.

The Initiator: They are the one to recognize the problem. It can come from almost any department or business function. An accountant may recognize from a benchmarking exercise they are paying far too much for utilities. The loading dock worker may see a safety hazard in the way the docks are laid out. Consequently, the person who recognizes the problem is looking for a solution.

The Influencer: This person or group of people have a say in how the problem gets solved and who the lucky vendor might be. In manufacturing plants, influencers are plant engineers and maintenance workers. In family decisions, it could be the kids influencing where they vacation.

The User: Users are the recipients of the purchase. Even if the new vacuum is twice as efficient as the old one and looks cool, if it is too heavy or awkward for the kids to use (don't they vacuum your home?) or your mom can't lift it, it'll be going back to the store. Don's mom returned more than one vacuum for this very reason.

In another example, if the attorney can't easily figure out the new billing software so they can keep track of hours that need to be billed, the salesperson (and maybe the influencer) will be in the dog house.

The Gatekeeper: These folks manage the flow of information during the sales process. They try to limit contact between the buying team and the selling team. The gatekeeper can be the receptionist, administrative assistant, project manager or any other level employee. The professional salesperson is skilled at discovering who the gatekeeper is and providing for the needs of this person.

The Purchaser: Purchasers handle the negotiations for the sale and take care of the paperwork. In a large company, this might be the administrative assistant, buyer, purchasing agent or project engineer (among other titles).

In small buying teams, one player may have multiple roles. In large teams there may be more than one player in each role. By asking questions in the decision-making step, the successful salesperson builds a directory of who is playing what role.

Confirm Before You Move Ahead

Skilled sales professionals realize they may meet with team members individually as well as in groups. The team members' needs may not always be in sync. The great salesperson learns how to ask confirming questions to validate what they know from previous meetings and how to tactfully build consensus among all the players for their solution. For the presentation, where the salesperson asks for the order, they are adamant the Decision Maker and other key advocates are present to hear their solution. And the salesperson never accepts "I want to think it over" (more on this later).

When a sales professional and the buying team commit to working out a solution together, it's called "negotiated work." Obviously, this is the best situation for the salesperson. Sometimes there may be concurrent negotiations with two or more vendors, such as when the design for the new World Trade Center in New York City was developed. Over the course of the negotiations, the short list of acceptable vendors gets winnowed down to one finalist who then completes the project.

On the personal level, it's a lot like shopping for a new car, home or boat. Selling skills and application of the process are important. The successful salesperson quickly determines the source of the prospect's pain (or the reason he is interested in buying your product or service) and the benefit of eliminating it. They learn the budget and how the decision will be made before committing any energy into presenting a solution. The salesperson then uses the relationship they have built to leverage their position and win the sale.

Sealed-bid purchasing is common for large commercial projects, most local, state and federal government purchases, and even new home construction. The sealed bid from each hopeful vendor is prepared in accordance with a written specification. In theory, all the bids are of equal quality and the final decision is made based on the lowest price.

"Not a lot of selling going on here," you might say. But the key to being on the winning team lies not in the sealed bid itself but in the work done with the specification writer before the project is put out to bid.

There is also something called the "three bid" decision-making process. Many large construction projects, government purchases and corporate policies require receiving proposals, or bids, from multiple sources (often three). (We can debate the merits of creating competition rather than collaboration, but that's a topic for another book.)

Once you know this is the process, there are two choices: play their game or don't. To be successful in this environment, the selling process starts long before the project is known to the public. The key is to have your products in the bid specifications or at least have specifications written favoring your company over the competitors.

A new factory design may take several years to complete the specification process. During the specification development time, the wise subcontractor salesperson is working with the architect and engineer to get their products listed in the specification. If you are this successful salesperson, the competition will then be between the general contractors, not you and your competitors.

On many government bids, in order to make the bid process seem fair, they may list one or two vendors by name, then add the phrase "or approved equal." You can rest assured the skilled salesperson in this case has been involved with the specification writer to develop a specification to exclude most of their competitors. The specification would list features only their model has or a service their competitors can't economically provide. Some government specifications also have a "local content" requirement, such as: "The structural steel must be supplied by a company located within Rockingham County, Virginia."

Experienced salespeople know how to work the system to their benefit if the decision-making process is by sealed bid.

If you sell light fixtures, having your products listed by part number on the architectural design drawings assures that all the electrical contractors will include your products in their bid. The competition then becomes between the electrical contractors, not between you and your light-fixture competitors.

For instance, Don works with architects and engineers to have his employer listed as a primary vendor for custom-metal products in project specifications. When listed this way, he doesn't need to spend as much time running down bidders for each project; they are calling his company looking for prices to be included in their subcontract bid.

Labor unions can also be a source of special specifications. At one point in his career, Don sold safety products. Believe it or not, one item in the mix was Gatorade. Like sports athletes, industrial workers need to be hydrated when working in elevated temperatures.

The Kohler Company had employees working in hot environments, casting iron for bathtubs and firing ceramics for toilets and sinks. The union contract under which Kohler worked specified each worker was to be supplied with a specific amount and flavor of Gatorade each day. So, despite the availability of equivalent products at a better price or packaged more conveniently, only Gatorade could be purchased by Kohler for its workers.

Here is an example from the B2C sector that might help you understand.

Assume you are a very successful salesperson and have decided to purchase land and build a custom-designed home. You'll probably hire an architect to draw the plans and write the bid specification, hoping to entice several builders to submit bids.

There are many aspects of the project you don't really care about: what brand of electrical wire is used, where they buy the lumber, or what manufacturer makes the sewer pipe. If you really enjoy cooking, however, you will have a particularly strong opinion about the kitchen cabinets and appliances. The wise (and informed) appliance salesperson will be contacting you and the architect early on in the project to have his model specified. All the builders will need to bid on the same model. The competition then is between the builders. The appliance company is assured the sale.

Challenge Yourself

1. Think about the purchasing process the buyers use when deciding to buy your product or service.

2. Write a description or draw a diagram of the process for each product or service you sell. (Okay, if all the decision processes are similar, you can do one diagram. But think about them separately to be sure there are not subtle differences between decision-making processes.)

3. List the job titles or descriptions of everyone on the customer's buying team.

4. What is their function on the team?

5. On a sheet of paper write the name of each project you are working on. Then write the strategy you will use to close the sale. Include specific actions for each member of the selling team together with a time line. Note what additional resources you need to close the sale and your plan for getting them.

CHAPTER EIGHT

The Six-Step Sales Process

Now that you know you have the temperament and basic skills for sales, let's discuss the sales process.

A process is an organized method for accomplishing a task or reaching a goal. Think about the activities you do daily. Each one has a process. In the morning you get up, shower, get dressed, fix and eat breakfast, brush your teeth, then head to work. Routines may vary from person to person.

Think about the usual tasks you do each day at work and how you would describe them to others. The best processes are repeatable and teachable.

The sales process can be described as a funnel with the large end at the top and the small outlet at the bottom. As you move through the qualifying process, the volume of potential buyers you deal with gets smaller and smaller until they emerge as customers for life.

In selling, it all starts at the beginning—with the lead. A "lead" is someone or a company you think might someday be interested in what you have to sell. Leads have not yet been verified to determine if they are good or bad.

To be successful, you need lots of leads because most leads do not turn into customers.

If you work for a large company, there may be a marketing department doing promotional activities to get leads for you. If you are the entire marketing and sales department in your company, it's all up to you.

Generating Leads

There are many ways to secure leads, and the method may be determined by the industry you serve. Some ways to get leads are:

- **Cold calls**. Cold calls involve contacting people you don't know and have not met to secure business from them. You may have an industry association membership list you are using for the contact information. The people you contact may or may not know about you and your company.

- **Direct mail campaigns**. Often referred to as "junk mail," direct mail campaigns are mailings sent through the traditional post. Usually, these campaigns would be designed and mailed by the marketing department of your company. The goal is to secure appointments for the sales staff or direct purchases through the business website or toll-free telephone number.

- **Email marketing**. Similar to direct mail, email marketing campaigns are sent to lists of potential customers with the goal of increasing sales.

- **Educational promotions**. Focusing on educating potential customers by speaking at industry meetings, publishing informative articles, or developing a newsletter with an educational component can be effective in generating leads and sales.

- **Testimonial and referral marketing**. Testimonial statements from current and past customers can be used effectively to generate interest. Simply asking your customers, business associates, and friends for referrals to potential clients can increase leads.

- **Events and networking**. Networking events, conferences, and trade shows provide an opportunity to talk to potential customers and gather leads.

Prospecting for Customers

When you have a lead, you are still many steps away from securing a new customer. In fact, each lead needs to be evaluated to determine whether it will become a prospect or whether it gets tossed in the trash bin, just like if you were prospecting for gold. Gold prospectors evaluate what's in their pan, tossing out the debris and keeping the gold.

A "prospect" is a company or person who closely fits the profile of your best customers. From past experience, you think there is a chance they will need your product or service now or in the future. At this point, because you have not qualified this prospect, you don't yet know enough to judge whether they are worth your effort to pursue.

Qualifying Your Prospects

Prospects need to be qualified. This step in the process eliminates those who, at this time, are not likely to purchase your product or service. The process also allows you to focus on the prospects most likely to lead to a sale.

There are many reasons to eliminate prospects at this early stage. A few reasons are:

- They don't have a need or a problem you can solve.
- They don't have money to spend.
- They are currently purchasing from your competitor, who happens to be their sister-in-law.
- Or some other obvious reason.

The heart and soul of the selling process is prospect qualification.

Three questions will tell you whether your prospect is qualified to do business with you:

1. Does the prospect have a problem for which you have a great solution?

2. Are you speaking with the person who makes the decision?

3. Do they have the budget for your solution?

When you can answer all three questions affirmatively, you have a qualified prospect.

Conversion

The next step in the selling process is to convert qualified prospects to customers. You do this by presenting your solution to their problem in a persuasive way.

What you do next depends on whether the buyer is a customer, or a customer for life. Will this sale be a one-time sale, or are there possibilities for additional sales in the future?

Think of a funnel cake. It starts out as a little bit of batter and is poured through a funnel.

The cook (salesperson) tends it, cooks it and places it lovingly on a plate. The cook then sprinkles powdered sugar all over it before it ends up in your hands. It's a process that begins with the funnel. What you pour in determines what you end up with.

It's the same for sales. You will need to be pouring in lots of batter (leads) to successfully sell your funnel cake (product).

There are all kinds of studies and statistics to define customer turnover, or customer attrition. The actual rate of turnover is unimportant. What salespeople need to be aware of is each year some portion of their customer base will disappear. Some will be wooed away by the competition; some will move; some will go out of business and, unfortunately, we will actually chase some away.

Replacing these sales with similar ones will keep you at the same level. To grow, you need not only replacements for the ones you lost but additional new customers. It's very important to keep filling the funnel or eventually you will have no customers. (And you won't have any funnel cake, either.)

Six Steps to Sales Success

The sales process below has a long history of success in many industries and in both B2C and B2B situations. Don learned this process from his mentor, Jim Wilson, who learned it from a sales trainer named Sandler.

This sales process helps you qualify your prospect, make your first sale, and develop customers for life.

Step 1 – Build rapport. People buy from people they like, know, and trust. Building rapport is essential. Learn about your prospect and develop a trusting relationship with them.

Step 2 – Find the pain. What's troubling the prospect and how much of a problem is it? If you find the pain (or the problem that needs to be solved), you can move to the next step, and you are a little bit closer to making the sale.

Step 3 – Determine the budget. Do they have enough money committed to solve the problem? No amount of persuasion can move a prospect to buy if they don't have the money to do so.

Step 4 – Find the decision maker. Who will make the decision to buy? Be sure to have all the players together when the time comes for this step.

Step 5 – Get the order. Show that your solution is the best one for their needs, and persuade the customer to buy your solution. Ask for the order and sign the paperwork.

Step 6 – Complete the post-sale activities. What needs to be done to create a customer for life? Do everything reasonable to keep the customer happy.

We'll look at each of these steps in depth in the next chapters.

Challenge Yourself

1. Think about the last five sales calls you made. What was the outcome of each? Analyze them by listing the sequence of events comprising the outcome.

2. Draw a diagram of your sales funnel.

3. Keep track for a month of the number of leads, prospects, qualified prospects and customers. Have the numbers changed since you began keeping records of the results?

4. Write down ways to:
   - Generate more leads.
   - Improve the quality of leads.
   - Convert more leads to sales.

CHAPTER NINE

Building Rapport

Think about this for a moment. When you meet someone new, how long does it take to get a first impression? Do you notice most of the time the first impression is the lasting impression?

The first 30 seconds of meeting a new prospect—whether in person or on the phone—are critical.

Oh sure, we'll make adjustments as we get to know the person better, but if we don't like them at first, most likely we won't make the effort to get to know them better.

"People remember how you make them feel before they remember what you do," says Christina Kunkle of Synergy Life and Wellness Coaching in Harrisonburg, Va., reminding us people buy from people they like.

The first meeting works both ways. If you don't like the prospect, chances are you'll not pursue business with them. In fact, we recommend you follow a different lead and give up on the ones you don't feel comfortable with.

One of the things Lois has noticed is saleswomen are sometimes so eager to make a sale—perhaps because they are often people pleasers who like to help others—they take on customers or clients they don't really like. Later, they find they should have paid attention to their gut instinct in the first place because the customers were either hard to work with, didn't pay them or were hard to satisfy. So pay attention to your gut!

Determining Your Prospect's Personality Type

Although we're all unique, we all have similarities in our personalities. One way to generalize is to pay attention to the different personality types.

There are many different ways to figure out what kind of a communicator or personality type someone is. For instance, there's the DISC® approach, a personality test that determines behavioral style. DISC stands for Dominance, Influence, Steadiness and Conscientiousness (Compliance), and these behavioral styles comprise four basic personality types.

Everyone has elements of each personality type, but they generally have one, or maybe two, making up their predominant personality traits.

Think of a chart with two axes (see illustration on next page). The vertical axis measures assertiveness. The scale is not absolute but relative, with less assertive at the bottom and more assertive on the top. The horizontal scale is responsiveness, running from least responsive at the left to greatest at the right.

The two axes crossing at their center points create four quadrants.

High Fast Pace ——— Assertiveness ——— Low Slower Pace	Low Task Oriented	High Relationship Oriented
High / Fast Pace	**DOMINANCE** **Goal:** Results, control **Fear:** Losing control; being taken advantage of **Strengths:** Likes fast pace, new activities, change and variety. Quick to act and creates a sense of urgency in others. Enjoys challenges and competition. Can move forcefully to get results. Uses direct, action-oriented approach to solve problems **Words that Describe Him/Her:** High ego strength, strong-willed, decisive, desires change, competitive, independent, practical (Negative: pushy, impatient, domineering, attacks first, tough, harsh)	**INFLUENCE** **Goal:** People involvement; recognition **Fear:** Rejection; Loss of approval **Strengths:** Likes to interact with many different types of people. Likes to express thoughts and feelings to others. Animated and enthusiastic in expression. Quick to adapt to new ideas and change. Seeks ways to interact positively in difficult situations. **Words that Describe Him/Her:** Emotional, enthusiastic, optimistic, persuasive, animated, talkative, people oriented, stimulating (Negative: disorganized, undisciplined, manipulative, excitable, reactive, vain)
Low / Slower Pace	**COMPLIANCE** **Goal:** Accuracy; order **Fear:** Criticism of performance; lack of standards **Strengths:** Analyzes situation or problems. Weighs the pros and cons. Values accuracy, quality and correctness. Systematic in approach to situations or activities. Tactful and diplomatic in interactions with others. Uses subtle or indirect approaches to resolving conflict. **Words that Describe Him/Her:** Perfectionist, sensitive, accurate, persistent, serious, needs information, orderly, cautious (Negative: picky, stuffy, critical, judgmental, fears criticism, slow to make decisions)	**STEADINESS** **Goal:** Security; stability **Fear:** Sudden change; losing security **Strengths:** Accepting of other people's ideas; likes to cooperate with others to get results. Willing to extend self to meet other people's needs. Works to create a predictable, stable environment. Good at calming upset people. **Words that Describe Him/Her:** Dependable, agreeable, supportive, accepts changes slowly, contented, calm, amiable, reserved (Negative: unsure, insecure, awkward, possessive, conforming, wishy-washy)
	——— Responsiveness ———	

The four personality types shown in the DISC quadrants are:

- **Drivers.** People who are very assertive and not responsive on a personal level we call "Drivers." They map into the upper left "Dominance" quadrant.

- **Expressives.** Moving clockwise, we find those who are highly responsive and assertive, the "Expressives," found in the upper right "Influence" quadrant.

- **Supportives.** In the lower right quadrant, we find those who are not assertive but are responsive, or the "Supportives" in the "Steadiness" section.

- **Analyticals.** The lower left "Compliance" quadrant shows the "Analyticals," and they like to move at a slower pace—they are both steady and nonassertive.

Take a look at the DISC figure on the previous page to see which personality type fits you best.

So why did we bring this up? If you are interested in getting someone to like you, the best way to deal with them is in the style they prefer.

Drivers are no-nonsense people. They don't care about your kids, your great aunt Matilda's flower garden, or anything but the problem they have. They are not rude; they are focused on what they want to achieve. Talking about the latest Cubs game won't build rapport with them.

At the other end of the spectrum, the Supportives want to know all about your kids, dogs, and personal life, and they will discuss most anything other than business for as long as you'll let them.

Expressives are "people people." They are interested in you and knowing all about you. But still being high on the dominance scale, they will control the conversation. These folks will love to talk but more about themselves than you.

That's okay; they respond well to open ended questions.

The Analyticals are a bit introverted. Low on both the dominance and assertiveness scales, they are all business but are polite about it. Not much for chit chat but are great at answering questions in detail to be sure you are clear of the answer. Plan to go slow with this personality type.

The best salespeople quickly figure out which personality type they are meeting and adjust their conversation to the situation. As we discuss sales techniques, we'll remind you to tailor the technique to the personality of your prospect.

Windows to the Soul

Another method of determining personality styles is to watch your prospects' expressions and where they focus their eyes when they communicate. Remember that we are not experts in these methods for determining personalities. Through years of experience, we have learned to use them as indicators of personality styles.

Highly Visual people, or people who learn through seeing, will look up. Auditory people, those who learn by listening, look toward their ears. And Kinesthetic people, who learn by touching and feeling, look down (sort of internally). A system of teaching Visual/Auditory/Kinesthetic people was introduced by psychologists in the 1920s. Howard Garner later described these types of learners in his book ***Frames of the Mind: The Theory of Multiple Intelligence*** (1983).

This same theory proved that people look one way when they "create" information and another way when they simply "retrieve" it. Not everyone looks the same way for these functions; each person has their own direction that they look when creating and when retrieving.

So if you can determine which personality type they are (Visual, Auditory, Kinesthetic) and then figure out which direction they look when they are retrieving information, you can usually also tell when they are lying! (That would be the direction they look when they create new ideas.)

Lois, for instance, is a Visual personality. She looks up when she answers questions—up and to the right for retrieving stored information and up and to the left when creating a new answer.

It takes a bit of questioning to determine which of these three personality descriptions fits someone; then you have to ask questions to see which way they look to create and which way they look to retrieve. Your retrieval questions have to be about information they have to access, or think about, to answer. Otherwise, they will simply rotely reply.

"Where were you born?" is unlikely to encourage a person to shift their eyes because the answer requires a rote response; they have answered this so many times, it becomes automatic. But "Where did you go on your last vacation?" or "How long have you worked for XYZ Company?" may work well because they probably have to think about the question before they answer.

Once you determine which direction you think they look when retrieving information, you can move on to asking questions they will need to answer creatively. Some questions that may require creativity are:

- "What country haven't you visited that you would especially like to see?"
- "What's the best thing about working at XYZ Company?"
- "If you won the lottery, what would you do first?"

Productive Questioning

Rapport-building and, indeed all selling, is about asking good, insightful questions and then listening to the response. Let's discuss the four most useful types of questions a professional salesperson can use. The four types of questions are:

- Open-ended questions
- Closed-ended questions
- Reversal questions
- Clarifying questions

Open-ended questions are by far the best questions we can use, not only in building rapport but throughout the qualifying process. Our goal in qualifying is to discover all we need to know to eventually close the deal.

Open-ended questions get the prospect talking. Remember, those Drivers and Analyticals/Compliants don't want to say much, so well-crafted open-ended questions are important when dealing with these personality types.

If you are doing all the talking, you won't learn much from the prospect.

Pretend you're on a blind date and you want to find out as much as possible about the person, but you want to maintain your own privacy until you decide if this potential relationship is worth your personal investment. What would you do? You'd keep them talking, wouldn't you? And it's not usually very hard to do because people love to talk about themselves.

So an open-ended question is a lot like the questions you'd ask to your blind date. It's a question requiring a substantial answer from the prospect. These questions can begin with "who," "what," "when," "where," "how," "what if," and sometimes "why." Open-ended questions can be posed as a statement as well: "Tell me about your most recent success." Or: "Paint me a picture of how you see your business in ten years."

An open-ended question like "How are you today?" might get a single word answer from Drivers or Analyticals like "Fine" or it might elicit a long discussion about all their aches and pains from Expressives/Influencers or Supportives.

Ask questions you think you can solve with your products or services. Try to stick to appropriate, specific questions like "What problems are you having with delivery?"

Closed-ended questions elicit a simple response. They typically begin with a verb: "Are you ready to buy?" or "Is it the red one or do you prefer the blue?" With those less-responsive personality types even expertly crafted open-ended questions can become closed-ended. If so, you'll probably have to ask many questions to understand the situation.

Closed-ended questions are useful when summarizing conversations. After presenting your impression ask, "Is that correct?"

Reversal questions. What do you do when you are asked a question by the prospect? If an answer at this time would benefit your sales-call goal, then answer it.

Otherwise, keep the prospect speaking about what you want to know by using the reversal technique. The art of reversing is answering a question with a question to keep the prospect speaking.

On the next page find an example of a simple reverse:

Prospect: "What can you do about this situation?"

Salesperson: "What would make you happy?"

The more common situation is when the customer wants to take control of your sales call. Too early in the process they may ask, "What's this going to cost?" A polite reverse to this is to first offer a softening statement: "That's a very good question, but first, I need to ask you a couple more questions to determine what it might cost. Okay?"

In other cases, a question might come out of the blue:

Prospect: "Does your product come with a 100% unlimited, lifetime, transferrable warranty?"

Salesperson: (softening first) "That's a very good question." (reversing) "Why do you ask?"

Prospect: "The last time I bought one of these whimmydiddles from your competitor it broke after two months and they didn't do anything to help me out."

Now the salesperson has several new pieces of knowledge to be used at the appropriate time in closing this sale.

Clarifying questions are asked to be sure you heard the prospect correctly. They are formed by repeating or rephrasing what you heard and asking for agreement.

For example:

Salesperson: "Jacquie, what I heard you say was the most important thing of all is your new home be in a good school district. Is that correct?"

The Value of Rapport

We were having breakfast at a local diner with a couple of friends and discussing this book. Ken, a small business owner, offered this story: One day a nicely dressed, pleasant young woman, came in to Ken's business to sell office supplies. The young woman was full of energy and enthusiasm, which she readily shared with everyone she met in Ken's office. Ken thought she was rather short on the knowledge of her products; nevertheless, he bought $400 worth of office supplies from her—enough to carry his business for six to eight months.

We asked Ken why he made this buying decision. Ken said office products salespeople often come into his office. He felt most of them are more interested in talking about themselves and their products than finding out what his needs are. This woman paid attention, and she showed an interest in his business and what office products he needed to be efficient.

The lesson here is even though the seller had an undifferentiated commodity product, she made the sale because she got Ken to like her.

That's what the Rapport step is all about. Remember, people do business with people they like, know and trust.

Treat Everyone With Respect

Here's one of Lois's stories showing you how ***not*** to build rapport. It's part of the story Don told earlier about buying the Porsche Boxter. As you read this, think about how you could correct the problem if you were the business owner.

A few years ago, we went looking for an additional car. We were in the market for a fun little sports car. We thought getting a two-seater, sporty convertible would be a pretty good way to take care of Don's "midlife crisis."

Anyway, we stopped at a nearby dealership first because Don was interested in seeing the manufacturer's new two-seater sports car model. A salesman came up to us, offered his hand to Don, and said, "Hi. I'm Laurence Hobbit (name changed to protect the guilty), and you are?"

Don shook his hand and replied, "Don Crawford."

Lois put out her hand and said, "Hi, I'm Lois Carter Crawford." At first, the salesman totally ignored her. Then he did a double-take and finally shook her hand. It was a good 20 to 30 seconds delay. ***Lois was steaming!***

Don and Lois both knew the salesman totally blew it. (We don't think Laurence had a clue.)

Because what the salesman didn't know is Don may be the primary driver of the car, but he would never buy a car from someone who didn't treat Lois with respect.

In fact, Don didn't even consider buying a car there. He knows if he did, every time Lois got into the car, she'd be angry, and say, "I can't believe you bought this car from the salesman who treated me so poorly!"

Don's a pretty smart guy. He's not going to ruin his fun time by buying from a guy who treated Lois as if she didn't exist. So he said, "Thanks for your time," and we moved on.

We went to two other dealerships where both salesmen were smart enough to acknowledge Lois. In fact, the salesman at one business really catered to her and subsequently won the sale. (Smart guy.)

Without much effort, he sold us a Porsche Boxster convertible. The salesman bent over backwards to let us check out the car, too. We took it out for a drive for about an hour. And it was like the good old days—no salesman rode with us to listen to our every word and make sure we didn't steal the car. We drove it alone. (Fast! With the top down.)

Most people don't complain to the offender or his supervisor. They tell everyone they see about your poor customer service—maybe 250 people before they get tired of talking about it. Comments like this would be pretty bad for your business, wouldn't it?

And today, the damage can be much worse. Because every day, customers who feel they've been mistreated not only tell everyone they know about the problem, they often start to comment about it on social media, publish articles in local newspapers, and write about the experience in their newsletters or books like we have (although we didn't name the culprit). It's picked up by others, spreading like a cold virus. Soon your reputation is in the toilet.

What could the first dealership do to solve the problem? Probably not much. But a personal phone call would be a step in the right direction.

Deal with the Issues

If an issue might jeopardize building a beneficial relationship with a prospect, you need to take care of it efficiently.

We encourage you to clear up past problems right away. If you or your company failed in some way in the past, bring the subject up early during your sales call and clear the air.

Perhaps there has been negative news about your product, company or industry, or you are working to renew a relationship with a "fallen" customer. It's better to take care of an issue before you invest a lot of time and energy.

The prospect can easily turn one tiny problem into a fatal objection. Here's an example:

Salesperson: Mr. Poe, I was looking back in our records and noticed that until several years ago Poe's Print Shop was among our best customers. I did some research and found the reason we failed to keep you as a customer had to do with errors in billing. Is this your recollection?

Prospect: Yes, we had a period where it seemed every invoice we got from your company had an error. It was frustrating and time-consuming for us so we took our business elsewhere.

Salesperson: Mr. Poe, I can see how our poor performance cost us your business. If I could show you we have solved the problem with new technology, would you be able to put the experience behind you?

Prospect: Yes. I'm impressed you have the courage to come calling again. Let's talk about the changes you have made.

Here, the salesperson is not defensive. She accepts responsibility for the company's errors. She has an agreement to put aside past performance. Now she can get on with the sales process. Customers like to be heard and understood!

The next step in the sales process is finding the pain. We will discuss this important subject in the next chapter.

Challenge Yourself

1. Think about your ten best customers. Describe the relationship you have with each of them. Write down why you think they are your best customers.

2. Think about your ten most difficult-to-deal-with customers. Write down why each of them is a problem for you. How will you convert them to one of your best customers?

3. Use the DISC personality trait chart to locate where your dominant style is. Now use a green marker to indicate on the chart each of your best customers and a red marker to indicate your worst customers. What pattern do you see here?

4. At the end of each sales call over the next month, recall the number of open-ended and closed-ended questions you used. Write your recollection of the effectiveness of each during the sales call.

5. After each sales call, evaluate your performance and track how it changes over the month.

CHAPTER TEN

Finding the Pain

What do you think people's greatest fear is?

Dr. Michael Telch and the Laboratory for the Study of Anxiety Disorders (LSAD) in the Department of Psychology at the University of Texas at Austin have researched treatments for anxiety disorders since 1988, according to an article on the University website. "The biggest fear is public speaking, with 15 percent of Americans experiencing a dramatic fear of it," he said. "People have had to turn down jobs, and certainly students have dropped classes because of it."

The second greatest fear people have is the fear of change. Your job is to show the prospect that the pain of staying the same is greater than the pain of change.

But there must be pain to effect a change.

Be the Solution to Your Prospect's Pain

Why do we call it "pain," and not "want," "need," or "desire?" We call it pain to make a point—pain evokes an emotional response and all sales are made emotionally.

Yes, even if you think about the largest deals where mega companies are buying other mega companies, emotion is involved. It could be ego on the part of the chief executive officer or it could be fear of the future driving the acquisition.

In a personal sale, if the new suit doesn't make you feel good, you won't buy it. The purchase decision is made emotionally and justified analytically after the decision is made.

We know that prospects either have pain or the professional salesperson needs to put them in pain. There are three options:

- Your prospects have pain and know it.
- Your prospects think they have pain.
- Your prospects don't know they have pain.

No matter which option fits your prospect, your next step in qualifying is to get the pain out on the table. You cannot provide a solution unless you discuss your prospect's pain.

In his book ***SPIN Selling***, Neil Rackham describes an excellent process for getting to the pain and increasing it to an intolerable level. SPIN is an acronym for four types of questions to ask:

- **S**ituation
- **P**roblem
- **I**mplication
- **N**eeds-payoff

Situation questions are the bridge from Rapport to Pain. They elicit from the prospect valuable information for determining whether or not a problem exists. The inexperienced salesperson asks way too many situation questions. For prospects with the Driver personality, this will turn them off quickly; for the Supportive, you may never get to the heart of their problem.

One technique Don's mentor Jim Wilson calls "Picasso" gets the prospect to paint the picture of how he sees the future. You can ask situation questions about the person, his business and his role in the business. Finding out his goals and aspirations is helpful in formulating your sales strategy and creating pain. A simple, yet effective, opening is, "Tell me how you are currently motivating your sales team." It's likely your prospect will paint the picture for you.

The follow-on problem question is, "Do you believe this method will produce maximum results over the long run?"

Problem questions seek to have the prospect identify dissatisfactions they have. The successful salesperson learns to ask more problem questions than situation questions. If you can't link a problem the customer has to a solution you can provide, you won't make a sale.

Problems don't necessarily rise to the level of pain needed to effect a change.

Implication questions, offering insight into why the prospect believes there is a problem, drive in the thorn to build the pain. You need to question the prospect who noted a problem to find out why they think there is one.

Probing with implication questions unearths the implied need behind the desire to change. These are questions like, "What is this problem costing you?" or "Why do you want to change this?" For business you can bet it has to do with costs, productivity, regulatory compliance and profits. For consumers, on the other hand, it may be ego, lifestyle, educational, security or health driven.

Here's a sample industrial sales opportunity discussion:

Prospect: "It takes one person almost a whole shift to unload this tablet coater by hand."

Salesperson (trying to understand why this is a concern): "How does the unloading time affect the productivity and costs associated with this product?"

Prospect: "We have one full-time person for each tablet machine at a cost of $60,000 per year each."

Salesperson (digging for the implied need): "If there were a way to eliminate one or more of those technicians, how would this change benefit your operation?"

Prospect: "We'd reduce our costs significantly if we only needed one technician to run all three machines."

Salesperson (clarifying and teasing with a solution): "So, if we could automate the unloading process, you'd be interested in knowing how?"

Prospect: "Yes, of course, and also what it might cost."

Salesperson (Implication question): "Automating the unloading will also reduce the total processing time. How might automation affect your department?"

Prospect: (realizing another benefit): "Hmm, we might be able to meet our production quota with fewer machines. This change would save additional resources."

Salesperson (implication question): "What would being able to reduce the number of machines and operators save your department?"

Prospect: (thinking out loud): "Well, let's see. We can save two operators at $120,000 per year, and I'd have to determine if there are other uses for the idle machines—or maybe the reduced cost might help increase demand. Automating is looking like a feasible option."

You can see from this simple example how the salesperson led the prospect to realize there is real value in making a change. On the other hand, for the prospect who didn't realize they had the problem in the first place a conversation might look like this:

Prospect: "I don't have much time to talk to you today. One of my staff is out ill and we've got an order to get out the door."

Salesperson (trying to understand this concern): "Wow! When one of your staff is unable to work, you lose a day of production? Our system can help you avoid losing production days. Would you be interested in discussing this idea soon?"

Used well, the implication questions drive the pain higher and higher to the point of agony. But salespeople are compassionate, so we won't let the prospect suffer—too long.

The needs-payoff question is the drug of choice to ease the pain. Needs-payoff questions point the prospect to hope. They build positive responses from the customer by focusing on solutions. Asked well, they'll allow the customer to catalog all the benefits that will accrue when the solution is implemented. Continuing the earlier conversation:

Salesperson (needs-payoff): "If you were to automate the unloading of these machines, you'd see several benefits, wouldn't you?"

Prospect: "Yes, we'd save labor costs and speed up the operation. Automation would decrease costs and increase capacity."

Salesperson (needs-payoff with a smile): "And review time is coming up soon. This kind of operational initiative would look good to your supervisor wouldn't it?"

Prospect: "Yes, indeed."

Salesperson (needs-payoff): "To design and fabricate the automatic unloader would take about 3 months. So you could begin implementing the savings this year. If we focused on improving productivity, what do you think the annual savings would be?"

Prospect: "Since productivity would triple, we'd only need one machine and operator, not three. So we'd save at least $120,000. I'm not sure what the operating cost reduction would be or opportunity for increased sales. Let me get back to you with those savings, okay?"

The best salespeople ask an increasing number of questions in each category.

- They ask only enough situation questions to find a problem.
- Then they ask several problem questions to validate it is a real problem.
- Next, they ask more implication questions to reinforce why the prospect thinks there is a problem.
- Finally, they ask more needs-payoff questions to direct the prospect to the value of solving the problem using their solution.

Thus pain is firmly established.

The top salespeople use the SPIN technique to uncover all the pain. Once they have identified a problem and worked it through the needs-payoff, they summarize what they have heard and get confirmation from the prospect. After they are certain all the pain has been uncovered and the prospect agrees what problem(s) needs to be solved now, the salesperson can move on to the budget step.

Remember not all people are in pain so it's your job to put them there. For example: A recruiter of high-level executives was asked how he was so successful in getting people who thought they were happy in their current positions to move to a new, uncertain future. His response: "They didn't know how unhappy they were until they met me!"

After the customer realizes they are in pain, you need to know if they have the budget to solve the problem. The next chapter will address this step in the selling process.

Challenge Yourself

1. Think back over the last month. Write down the pains your ten best customers had.

2. List the top ten problems your company solves for its customers.

3. Create a "pain scale" to use on each sales call. 0 = they are so happy with the current situation nothing could get them to change. 10=imminent disaster if they don't change right now.

4. For each sales call rate the customer's pain level at the beginning of the call and again at the end of the call. Think about what you did to change the pain level.

5. Before each sales call in the next month, rehearse the call using an imaginary conversation that includes all four categories of questions in the SPIN technique. At the end of each sales call evaluate your performance.

CHAPTER ELEVEN

Determining the Budget

The transition to discussing the budget is the natural progression following the implication and needs-payoff steps. In those steps you identified the cost of the problem. In the budget step, your goal is to determine the amount of money the prospect has to solve the problem.

By asking the implication questions you found out what the problem is costing the prospect and you have an idea what your solution will sell for. So, it's time to move on to asking the budget questions.

In B2B sales, discussing the budget is generally easier than when selling to consumers. Prospects find it easier to discuss their employer's budget than their personal budget.

After all, we humans are uncomfortable talking about our money—at least Americans are, especially if it is our personal money. If you don't like to discuss money, then you'll have a hard time talking about it with your prospects. This can be a major hurdle to get over, and you will have to practice talking about money to be able to easily do it.

Continuing from the example in Chapter 10:

Salesperson (summarizing): "We agree you'll save at least $120,000 per year once the automatic unloader is in operation. What are you willing to invest to gain this savings?"

Prospect: "Hmm. We can easily get funds approved when we show a one-year payback and often we can make these kinds of operating improvements with a three-year payback as well."

Salesperson (confirming): "Then if the price for the project came in between $120,000 and $360,000 you'd be able to get it funded?"

Prospect: "Obviously we'd like to be closer to the $120,000 than the upper end. It would make funding more likely."

So now you know the target number the prospect has in mind. There are three possible circumstances:

- His budget is what's needed to solve the problem.
- The budget is more than adequate.
- The budget is woefully short.

Before you leave the budget step, address the relationship between their budget and your price. If the budget is spot on to what it would cost, you can simply say, "I think we can solve your problem and get a one-year payback."

Suppose you know the solution is only half of the budgeted number? Then when you make your presentation, bundle in some value-added services—like a maintenance agreement—to make the customer feel well-cared for. In a follow-on sales call you can discuss what other products or services he might need to purchase from you.

The tough part comes when the budget isn't sufficient to solve the problem. If you know the budget isn't sufficient, the time to discuss the budget issue is ***now***.

There are two choices: Either you can redefine the scope of work to meet the funds available or you can help the customer find additional money. Where do those funds come from? Work with the customer to determine the solution. You'll need to ask questions and reinforce the needs-payoff.

Say the solution was $500,000 in the above example. Here's how the conversation might go:

Salesperson (softening the blow): "I can see why you'd like the solution to be in the $120,000 to $360,000 range. What would happen if it was higher?"

Prospect: "Well, I'd have to spend more effort in preparing the request for funding. Then it would need to be approved at another level, maybe two, in the company."

Salesperson: "Didn't you say there would be other savings besides the labor costs?"

Prospect: "Yes, but it takes some time and effort to get the accounting and operating folks to generate those estimates."

Salesperson: "It's going to take me two-to-three weeks to get a proposal together for you. Is this time period enough to gather the other savings numbers?"

Prospect: "Yes. Then perhaps we can get this project underway before my next review."

Okay, we have the budget number to work with and we've gotten the commitment from the prospect. Now we need to understand how decisions are made.

Challenge Yourself

1. What is your comfort level with discussing money?

2. In your personal purchases, how does money influence your buying decision?

3. How does your personal attitude about money affect your sales success rate?

4. Think about your top ten customers. How much of an issue is the price of your product or service to them?

5. When you discuss price, how do you persuade your customers of the value of your product or service?

6. Track your performance for each sales call for a month. When the prospect says: "Your price is too high," evaluate how you handle those situations.

CHAPTER TWELVE

Finding the Decision Maker

In consumer purchases, the decision maker is usually only one person. Sometimes another family member or two are also brought in.

When selling to businesses, the decision-making process is more complex. Group decision-making has some or all of the following players:

- The Decision Maker (they control the budget and have profit and loss responsibility)
- The User (they are the ones who will put the product or service to work)
- The Influencer (these people don't make the decision but can be advocates for or antagonists against you)
- The Purchasing Agent (they do the paperwork and put the transaction into effect on behalf of the Decision Maker)
- And there may be others who provide input (consultants, engineers, lawyers, owners, etc.)

Everyone who uses your product has a different relationship with it. Consider this example from a sales rep friend of ours working the printing industry:

"If you are calling on a large healthcare system, as I do, there may be multiple department heads affected by your product. For instance, selling patient wrist bands: The admitting department will be printing and applying them, so you will want to ask how they run through the printer, how they are applied to the patient's wrist and what it would mean if you could improve the process or product," says Jane Missel, sales consultant.

"Then you may talk with the nursing staff to see how they scan the bar code on the wrist band, and you ask about patient comfort. Each constituent has a different measure of what makes a good product," she says. "They all want to know, 'What's in it for me?' The successful salesperson will include all those benefits in their presentation."

Why is it important to know how decisions are made?

Picture this: You spend one or two meetings with your prospect creating pain and establishing a budget. If you present at this time and they can't commit, where are you? Back to square one or worse—out of the picture if your competition has been pitching to the decision maker. When you pitch at the lower level, you also risk losing the sale if your unqualified prospect tries to sell the idea to the decision maker and does a poor job.

Your goal in understanding the decision-making process is to find out who the decision maker is and how decisions to purchase your solution are made. Then you have to get in front of the decision maker to do your pitch, if at all possible.

Consider the simple case of husband and wife looking for a new car. As the car salesperson, you may have met with the husband, built rapport, found out why he wants a car, determined his budget and even gotten his commitment that he has found the car of his dreams.

Then, when you try to close the deal, you feel the cold slap in the face when he says, "Of course, my wife needs to agree." What a waste of time when early on in the process you could have asked how the decision would be made and gotten the wife involved right from the beginning.

How do you find out who the true decision maker might be without offending your prospect? One simple question to ask is, "In addition to yourself, who else might be involved in deciding to purchase this solution?" Tailor it to suit your style, but keep it professional and acknowledge the role of your prospect.

From the previous B2B example of the automatic unloader machine, we already know there will be another level or two of approval required. Here's how the conversation might have gone:

Salesperson (transitioning from budget to decision): "You mentioned others would have to approve this project. Could you describe the process?"

Prospect: "Yes, I assemble the request for funds, including your proposal and my justification, payback and recommendation. Then I pass this on to my boss, Mr. Jones. If he approves it, then it would go to purchasing where an order would be issued. Again, if the payback is greater than one year, it'll have to be sent over to division for their approval at a capital review meeting."

Salesperson: "When's the next review meeting?"

Prospect: "There was one several weeks ago, so if I get the request approved by my boss, it'll get on the agenda for next month's meeting. Otherwise it will be close to six months from now."

Salesperson: "Can we schedule a meeting with you and your boss in a couple of weeks to review my proposal?"

This is the time the professional salesperson fights to get in front of the decision maker along with the prospect who is recommending your solution. Should the prospect object, you can offer reasons to be included, for example:

- Convince the prospect you would be an asset able to answer all the boss's questions and help the prospect to look good in front of his boss. This prevents the prospect from appearing unprepared and jeopardizing the sale.
- If it's a particularly complex product, offer to bring your technical team along and have his technical team involved as well to make sure all necessary questions are answered.

As you present your appeal, keep in mind your prospect has a vested interest in solving the problem and eliminating the pain. Your task is to convince him you are better qualified to present your solution than he is, and the solution will only make him look good.

There are situations where the decision-making process is completely out of your control.

Public bids where proposals are submitted sealed, and opened and read at the appointed time.

Reverse auctions, once popular with large corporations, where vendors compete electronically by putting in a bid for the project. The lowest bid amount is then shown to all bidders who have a chance to beat it. (We think this is a no-win process. And indeed has almost disappeared.)

Capital purchases review meetings, as in the example above discussing the automatic unloader, only look at paperwork to make an approval decision. It would be up to the prospect's boss to present the proposal at the meeting. It is unlikely you (as the salesperson) would be involved at this level.

When you know the decision-making process, you can then determine whether or not to pursue the sale.

When you have a clear understanding of the decision-making process, the budget, and the pain, you finally have a qualified prospect. You also have all the information you need to make a compelling presentation.

Let's talk about getting the order. Chapter 13 discusses this step in the selling process.

Challenge Yourself

1. For each of your top ten customers, list the title of the person who makes the purchasing decision.

2. For the ten worst sales calls you have made in the last month, evaluate your effectiveness in getting to the decision maker.

3. Rate your comfort level in selling to C-level executives (chief executive officer, chief information officer, chief financial officer, etc.). Are you at ease working with these folks or are you nervous when dealing with people "above your pay grade?"

4. Does it make a difference whether the decision maker is a man or woman?

5. Is there a difference whether it is a large or small business?

6. Does the age of the decision maker affect how you deal with them?

CHAPTER THIRTEEN

Getting the Order

Now that you've built rapport, found your prospect's pain, discovered the budget, and established the decision maker, it's time to make the presentation.

But the presentation doesn't come free to the prospect. No, you don't invoice them for your time (usually); they "pay" by making a commitment to you.

What is it you want out of the presentation? That's right, your top priority is a direct purchase or a purchase order, depending on the way it is done in your industry.

You want the prospect to listen to your pitch, give you an honest appraisal and tell you "Yes."

The only other acceptable option is for the prospect to tell you "No." With a "No" you have a chance to understand the reasons behind the "No," and go on selling.

The death knell is: "I want to think it over" (IWTTIO). Truth be told, the only person thinking about it is you.

Where are you if you get IWTTIO? In limbo. What do you do next? Invest more time in this prospect, trying to make a sale that may never happen.

And what happens when you continue to chase the sale? Prospect responses to your efforts may vary for a number of reasons, such as their personality type, company culture or cultural heritage.

Responses Based on Personality Type

You can call and leave messages on their voice mail, which are never returned. If the solution doesn't fit, Driver and Analytical personality people will be more likely to be straight forward and tell you, "No." The Expressive and Supportive folks are too people-oriented, and they don't want to hurt your feelings, so they will likely avoid your calls.

Differences in Culture

Getting IWTTIO can be cultural as well. Some cultures simply don't believe it's polite to say, "No thanks." Or they may want to take the easy way out by avoiding saying no.

The folks in the Northeast U.S. are more direct than the genteel South. In the North, it's likely your prospect will tell you they aren't interested. Down South, however, when someone says, "Sweetie, you've done a great job. And I can see lots of potential in what you're saying, but I'll have to think it over" (or "let's get together again sometime"), it's really a polite "No." In fact, they may even say, "Thank you. You've done a wonderful job here, and we'll take you up on your offer." And it still means "No, thanks!"

If they haven't signed on the dotted line or given you a check, you don't have a "Yes."

How to Avoid IWTTIO

Your task ***before*** you make the presentation is to get a commitment either a "Yes" or a "No."

One way to assure a definitive choice is to say with confidence (speaking to the decision maker):

"Robert, I have a good understanding of your problem and what it's costing you. I think we can propose a solution to fit your budget. When we meet again next week, I have a favor to ask. If you like what I present, would you be able to commit to a purchase immediately?

"And if you don't think my solution will work, would you have a problem saying so?" . . . "Then we agree. At the end of my presentation, I'll either hear a 'Yes' or a 'No' from you—no 'think it over's,' right?"

Script this conversation to fit your own style and practice it until it sounds natural. It's likely you will have to say this to many prospects during your career.

Let's review the sales process thus far:

- You spent the time building rapport and getting the prospect to like you.
- You have identified several problems severe enough to cause them to change.
- With deft questioning, you found they have enough money set aside to solve the problem.
- You have identified the decision maker, the other players and how they make the purchase decisions.
- And you have a commitment for a thumbs up or down when you make your presentation.

Now you have a well-qualified prospect.

The Effect of Sales Cycles

Let's talk about sales cycles. In short sales cycles for minor purchases made by a single decision maker, this whole process could take only a few minutes to get to this point. For major purchases of complex solutions, it could be months or years to qualify the prospect. It all depends on your product or service, the industry you are in, and your skill in applying the process.

The Presentation

Once you have the prospect qualified, it's time to invest in the presentation.

For some products sold on a one-call close (that is, during the initial phone call or in-person meeting), the presentation immediately follows the qualification. For others, a formal presentation needs to be prepared.

The presentation is not a time for you to demonstrate your vast knowledge of your product, the prospect's company, the industry they are in and the worldwide economy. When you do a good job of qualifying, the prospect gives you all the information you need to close the sale.

Look at what you know:

- The problem
- How it affects the prospect's business
- Their perceived benefit from eliminating the problem
- What they are willing to spend to make it go away
- And how they will decide to purchase your solution

The presentation, whether formal or informal, written or spoken, has three parts:

1. **Recap and confirm the pain.** Begin with summarizing the problem and its implication (remind them of the pain), and get concurrence you are correct. Remind them of the benefits of solving the problem and the savings by ridding themselves of it. Get agreement on the budget they have to solve the problem and then repeat the commitment for a "Yes" or "No." If, at any point here, the feedback from the customer doesn't agree with your perception of the situation, stop and clear up any misconceptions before moving on.
2. **Present your solution.** Tailor your argument using only the features and benefits of interest to ***this*** prospect. Features are the unique aspects of a product or service that make it stand out from your competitors, describing what it is. Benefits are the reasons the prospect should buy your product or service, answering: "What's in it for me?"
3. **Close the order.** When you complete your presentation, ask for the order. More sales are lost when the salesperson doesn't ***ask*** for the sale than for any other reason.

Use Your Advantage

Here's an excellent example about differentiating yourself from others:

"Every once in a while, in a competitive environment, a good salesman should not feel compelled to 'play fair.' If you have a connection or feature that others cannot match, use it. Our museum was in competition with a fancy country club and a hotel to host a big alumni event for my alma mater, Virginia Military Institute (VMI). Catering, parking, and ambiance were close. So I let VMI know that I did not intend to play fair. I offered to put on a special exhibit during their event that featured Civil War artifacts from famous soldiers with VMI connections—the sword and shoulder epaulets from Stonewall Jackson's VMI uniform; the sword of Walter Taylor, VMI graduate and Robert E. Lee's chief-of-staff; the sword of John Quincy Marr, VMI grad and the first Confederate officer killed in the war; and several other items. I then challenged the competitors to match us. It cost us nothing, but it won us the contract," says S. Waite Rawls III, president, The American Civil War Museum Foundation.

Getting to Yes

Remember that if it's a complex solution, during the presentation you should frequently stop and query the decision maker and his associates, making sure they understand and are in agreement. Here's where your presentation skills come in. There will be questions. Don't think of these interruptions as objections. They will be points needing clarification. Remember, by asking questions along the way (that are answered in a positive way), you are leading the customer to that last positive response: YES!

The purpose of the presentation is to get a "Yes" from the prospect and turn him into a customer. When you get the "Yes," the next two words you say are: "Thank you."

Now, ***stop selling***. That part of the job is done. Should you keep presenting past this point, you risk losing the sale.

But what if the answer is "No?" Your challenge at this time is finding out why the answer is "No." Some people think the "No" is merely an objection. In our experience, it usually means something has not been made clear to the customer.

Now it's time to answer those questions. You will need to assess if the question is a genuine concern or a smoke screen.

Here's where probing questions come in handy. You need to ask enough questions to be sure the objection is a legitimate barrier to the prospect issuing an order.

This is also "gut check" time. You are a good enough judge of human nature; you can determine whether the prospect is simply being polite and is offering a gentle out for himself or if he does want to buy but has serious questions about your solution.

Once you understand the question and believe it is legitimate, restate the concern to the prospect to get confirmation you do understand it correctly. Then address the concern. When you are finished, get confirmation the objection has been cleared away.

And again ask for the order.

The most common objection in the world is, "Your price is too high." If you have worked the system well using the SPIN technique discussed earlier, then the likelihood of this objection is low unless the prospect is comparing your offer with others. When this happens, the prospect believes he is buying a commodity (or something that is exactly the same no matter where you buy it). If you haven't differentiated your offer (and your company) from the competition early on, then it's difficult to overcome the commoditization of your product or service.

Other concerns come from you not understanding the problem or the decision-making process. Sometimes situations change between the time you first met to discuss the pain and the time you present. In this case, you need to go back to the qualification process and work it again.

Our experience with this system is we rarely have to present. When we have started the process with the correct decision maker, by the time we get through the needs payoff, the prospect is ready to buy. So pay attention throughout the process for those buying signals (we will discuss this more in Chapter 21) and take advantage of them. Ask for the order.

Now that you made the sale, what happens? And what do you need to do? We will discuss post sale secrets and activities in the next chapter.

Challenge Yourself

1. Think back over the last month. How many IWTTIO's did you get?

2. List your top ten customers and describe the sales cycle for each of them.

3. Over the last month think about the sales you lost. When did you enter the sales cycle for each of them (beginning, mid-point, close to the end)?

4. When you present, do specific objections or concerns come up frequently? List them. After you have completed the list, work to include these topics and their solutions early in the sales process for each prospect.

CHAPTER FOURTEEN

Post Sale Secrets & Activities

After the "thank you," the post-sale step in the process begins. The most important task in the post-sale is to make sure the order sticks. If you have ever had the "Yes" taken away unexpectedly, you know how disappointing it can be.

In 1997, Don was developing new business with the safety department of a large paper mill. The safety director was interested in purchasing five breathing air carts. Don came in after the competition had given their presentation and quoted list price for each of the carts. He shared that at the five-unit price, there was a quantity discount of about 25 percent, no small amount on a total order of $125,000. The safety director appreciated his effort and sent the requisition to the purchasing department.

Several days later Don followed up with the buyer. He'll never forget what she said, "Oh, I called the first vendor to see if they would offer the quantity discount, too. When they did, I placed the order with them. Don't you think that was fair? Wouldn't you like the same consideration?"

The first time something like this happens to you, you probably won't be prepared.

Don wasn't either.

Don was too shocked at the arrogance of the buyer to remember what he said, but it was probably a milquetoast response like, "Well, yeah." What he should have said was, "Hmm, that's an interesting approach to buying. Reward the company that was going to make you pay full price until I came along. So no, I don't think that was fair."

Better yet, if Don had rehearsed the prospect, this situation wouldn't have happened this way. Rehearsal is taking the buyer through a scenario of what might happen before it occurs.

Here's what Don says now in situations like the example above: "Mr. Buyer, I know you have a price from my competitor, and she is a competent saleswoman. When she calls and you tell her I had a lower price, she'll probably ask for a second look. How will we handle this situation?"

Note that Don said ***we*** in this example. Using "we" confirms to the customer that the prospect and the salesperson are in this together now.

Use the rehearsal technique whenever you suspect the buyer may have cause to reverse their decision or to be overcome by buyer's remorse. Here's an example: "Mr. and Ms. Buyer, you have purchased a beautiful, new, state-of-the-art refrigerator. It will be delivered in a couple of days. In the meantime you may wonder whether or not you bought the right refrigerator. When that happens, would you call me, please? Then we'll work through any concerns together."

Remember, all purchase decisions are emotional, and then we justify them rationally.

Buyer's remorse comes in the justification stage. If there is concern, you want to be there to help them remember the pain, the implication and the needs-payoff.

In addition to making sure the deal is closed, there are other post-sale tasks. Fulfillment is the most important. You need to be sure your company delivers on the commitment and the customer is pleased.

Sometimes in small sales the product or service is delivered immediately, like a massage or a haircut. Other times it may take a while, like new windows, a machine tool or a new factory. The salesperson's role is to stay involved to make sure the customer is happy.

Of course, with a little creativity, you can make them happy and create better sales for yourself. That's what our daughter Veronica did.

"My sales always rank first or second, even though I only work breakfast and lunch. For awhile, my supervisor scheduled me in the smallest section of the restaurant, which meant I had to work more days to make the same amount of money. I didn't want to do that, so I started selling the dinner menu at lunch. I point out the more expensive dinner options, and then offhandedly say, 'And this is the lunch menu.' They choose a meal from the dinner menu, and, of course, they have to have a glass of wine or another bar item along with their meal," says Veronica Enright, restaurant server.

With each sale there are three possible outcomes: moment of truth, moment of misery or moment of magic:

- A moment of truth happens when the delivered service or product meets the customer's expectations.

- A moment of magic is when the customer's expectation is exceeded. Moments of magic create customers for life. They will be loyal to you and avoid the predatory competitors who seek to take away your hard-earned business.
- A moment of misery occurs when expectations are not met. It is most important for the salesperson to stay involved to change those moments of misery into moments of truth, at least, or better yet, moments of magic.

Seth Godin, author of several customer relationship and marketing books including ***Purple Cow***, calls this "creating customer evangelists," or people who love you so much they spread the good word about you.

When we bought our Porsche Boxster, the owner of the dealership filled out a "we-owe" list. Some things on the list, like an owner's manual, were to be delivered soon; others were to be done at the first service, "which, by the way will be free to you," he said. Wow, it was a moment of magic for us and a good value to the dealership owner. He received several referrals from us and sold at least one other car before we even had the first service!

Post-sale activities also set you up for the next sale. This is the time to begin the cycle all over again, looking at the situation anew. The next sale can come from this customer or ones they refer to you.

If you ask, you'll get referrals and testimonials, i.e., letters or statements saying how happy they are with you, that you can use to secure more customers.

These referrals can be to prospects outside of the customer's own organization or family, as well as from inside the organization. Don, who sells specially designed and crafted metal solutions, has been quite successful "selling deeper" into a new customer's company by getting immediate referrals to others in the company from his new customers. This works well with large construction companies running many projects and multiple offices or any business with multiple locations with similar problems.

Once his company's craftsmen produce a moment of magic, Don asks the customer to introduce him to other project managers who would have a need for similar product.

Don continues to maintain the current customer relationship while also pursuing these referrals. He keeps the customer informed about his success with the referrals they gave him as well. We will talk more about customer relationship management in Chapter 22.

Stick to the Process

To summarize, there are six steps in the sales process. If you follow the process, it will work for you, saving time, making you more productive, and creating the outcomes you desire. Remember these six steps:

1. Build rapport.
2. Find the pain.
3. Determine the budget.
4. Identify the decision maker and influencers.
5. Get the order.
6. Assure post-sale behaviors and activities.

Just a reminder, when you fulfill the order and deliver on your promises, remember to ask for testimonials you can share with potential customers, as well as referrals from your happy customer.

Now that you understand the overall sales process, it's time to put it into practice. There are many activities that comprise the sales process steps. In the coming chapters we will go into several of these activities.

In the next chapter, we will discuss more about finding and identifying qualified prospects, and an important activity in the selling continuum, setting an appointment with a prospect.

Challenge Yourself

1. Are there situations when you lose the sale after the customer says "yes?" If so, write down your recollection of each situation. Is there something in common here?

2. Over the next month, concentrate on rehearsing your customer on what to expect during the fulfillment phase. Evaluate the effect this has on creating happy, life-long customers.

3. For each of the solutions you sell, create a list of follow-on products or services to increase the value of the customer.

4. After the product or service has been delivered, follow up with your customer to determine his level of satisfaction.

5. Think back over the last month. How many sales resulted in moments of magic? How many referrals did you get from each of them? Over the last month, how many moments of misery did your customers experience? For each one describe how you handled it and if you converted it to a moment of magic or at least a moment of truth.

CHAPTER FIFTEEN

Setting Appointments

Now that you understand the selling process, you're ready to go sell something. To do that, you will need an appointment with a qualified prospect.

How do you get your first appointment with Mr. Big? First, ask yourself, "Why would Mr. Big want to meet with me?"

List all the ways you can help him solve problems in his business using your product or service. Once you have this list of problems and solutions, you are prepared to pick up the phone and try to secure an appointment.

Remember, with this activity, the goal is to get an appointment, not sell the product or service.

When you set appointments, they are with unqualified prospects (or "suspects"), qualified prospects who are at some point in the sales process, or customers—basically either folks who don't know you or people who do know you.

Getting through the "noise" that comprises people's lives today will likely be your biggest challenge, but we have a few ideas to help you connect and secure appointments.

Prospects Who Don't Know You

Let's start with those who don't know you. These could be leads from your marketing department, ones you have identified yourself, or referrals from customers.

Use the telephone to set the first appointment. Since this is the first contact you have with a new prospect, this is the time to begin building rapport. Our general rule is never to leave a message but to keep calling until you reach the person. It's tough in today's business environment in which everyone has caller ID and voice mail, but do you best.

Yes, this is a high-tech world today, but remember first the prospect has to like us. We begin building that rapport with the first contact. A personal phone call allows you to have a dynamic conversation where you can evaluate the prospect.

Some ways to successfully reach a prospect by phone are:

- Call at various times of the day. Before or after regular business hours are generally good times to call owners and managers. Immediately before, during or after lunch can be good times for any prospect as well.
- Call every day until you reach the person.
- Call the company's general number and talk to the receptionist. Ask this person to transfer you to the prospect.
- Call another person in the company you know and ask this person to put you in touch with the person you wish to meet.

Getting in touch with prospects (and customers!) is a challenge, but you can do it. Be creative and determined.

"The biggest issue for me today is every company seems to be doing more with less. People are busier than ever before and don't have time to see sales consultants. Using referrals and showing the advantages of meeting are key to getting the customer's attention. Sometimes it takes months to finally get someone on the phone. In one company I worked for, we called it 'polite persistence.' Show you are a valued consultant and you will help their company or business in some way. Be persistent, but don't be a pest," says Jane Missel, sales consultant.

Dealing with Receptionists

Receptionists are our favorite people. Treated with respect, they can be a great source of information (and they can either open the door for you or close it in your face).

If you know a company would benefit from your product or service, but you don't know the decision maker or influencers, receptionists can point you to the right people. If you phone asking for a person who is no longer with the company, the receptionist will get you to their replacement.

When the receptionist offers to send you to a person's voice mail, politely accept the offer—not with the intention of leaving a message, mind you, but to learn what you can. When this is a person you haven't met, at the very least, you can find out how they pronounce their name. This is gaining more importance as Asian, Eastern European and Arabic immigrants move up the U.S. corporate ladder to the role of decision makers.

The message may tell you they are out of the office for a while, so you'll know when to call back. They may give a cell phone number or refer you to another person.

You'll also learn whether they use their given name or a nickname. Your lead form may say Richard Conrad Reynolds IV, but he may go by "Buddy" or "Junior" or "Conrad." When you phone again, you'll sound more professional when you use his nickname.

Script the Call

No, you won't read your script like some bored telemarketer. You'll simply use it as a guide for the phone call. The purpose is to convince the prospect they need to meet with you.

Here's an example:

Salesperson: "Hello, may I please speak with David Jones?"

Prospect: "This is David."

Salesperson: "David, this is Sara from the Great Company. How are you today?"

Prospect: "Fine thanks."

Salesperson: "The Great Company provides a unique service to reduce your cost of light bulbs. David, are you the one who is responsible for purchasing light bulbs?"

Prospect: "Yes."

Salesperson: "Do you have a few minutes or is this a busy time?"

<u>Option 1:</u>

Prospect: "I'm in a meeting now. Can you call again?"

Salesperson: "Yes. I'm sorry to interrupt you. When would be a good time to phone back?"

Then set at time to call back, put it on your calendar and call when you said you would.

<u>Option 2:</u>

Prospect: Yes. I can talk now. What are you selling?

Salesperson: The Great Company has a service for maintaining light bulbs in large buildings like yours, proven to save 4 to 6 percent a year. I'd like to stop by and discuss the service with you. Would you have time to meet on Wednesday morning?

Prospect: Yes, Sara. Come on by at 9:45.

Salesperson: 9:45 it is, David. When I come by I'll take no more than 30 minutes to tell you about our company and light bulb program, and ask you a few questions about how you handle light bulbs now. Okay?

Prospect: Yes.

Salesperson: Thanks, David. I'll see you Wednesday morning at 9:45.

Let's break down Sara's call. First, she confirmed she was speaking to the right person. Then she determined David was indeed the correct buyer.

Sara showed respect for his time by asking, "Do you have a few minutes or is this a busy time?" This is a magical phrase. Use it like this on every call. It gives the purchaser the feeling they are in control. If they don't have time, you can set another phone appointment.

When David agreed to speak at this time, she offered a short description of a universal benefit her product provides. It is general enough to stimulate his curiosity, but it's not a "sales pitch."

Sara then offered a time convenient to her schedule. If David didn't have a clear calendar at the time she asked for, Sara could have negotiated a mutually satisfactory time. Next, she set the agenda for the sales call and got confirmation. Sometimes the purchaser will offer to bring others to the meeting as well, which indicates they are willing to invest time in learning about your offer.

Early in the call Sara could have heard from David that he wasn't the right person to speak with. If so, she simply asks who she should be speaking with and gets their contact information. Then she either gets transferred or calls the person directly.

If you are calling to set up an appointment with a referral, the opening might sound like this:

Salesperson: "Hello, may I please speak with David Jones?"

Prospect: "This is David."

Salesperson: "David, this is Sara from the Great Company. How are you today?"

Prospect: "Fine, thanks."

Salesperson: "Beverly Lumen from the Better Realty Group referred me to you."

Prospect: "Oh, yes. I remember Bev told me about you."

Salesperson: "Then you may know the Great Company provides a unique service that reduces your cost of light bulbs. David, Beverly said you are the one who is responsible for purchasing light bulbs. Is this right? Do you have a few minutes or is this a busy time? . . ."

It's fundamentally the same except you bring the referral source into the conversation. This changes you from a potential nuisance call to a valuable caller very quickly.

In either case, the appointment-setting phone call should take about three minutes. Remember the goal is to get an appointment, not to sell your product.

Should the prospect start asking specific questions about your product or service, remember to stick to the system. Establish pain first. Politely decline to answer detailed product questions at this time.

Consider using the "Reversal" technique discussed earlier. For example:

Prospect: "I heard you have an awesome guarantee for your service."

Salesperson (reversing): "Yes, we do. And I'd like to discuss it with you when we meet. Would that be okay?"

Or

Prospect: "How large is your company?"

Salesperson (reversing): "That's an interesting question. I don't get asked it often. Why do you ask?"

Prospect: "We only deal with large companies."

Salesperson: "I'll bring along the vitals on our company when we meet. We can discuss them then. Okay?"

There may be some simple questions you do want to answer:

Prospect: "Where are you located?"

Salesperson: "We are on Rockfish Boulevard. Do you know the area?" (Back to the purchaser)

Prospect: "Good. You're close enough to give good service." (Salesperson notes good service—whatever that means—is important.)

Setting appointments with those who already know you—either customers or prospects at some point in the selling process—has the same goal: setting an appointment, not trying to sell your product or service.

Cold calling is a special kind of appointment seeking. Because there is so much to it, we discuss it in depth in Chapter 17.

Setting Appointments with People You Know

One way to easily set appointments in a specified area with people you currently do business with is to use email. Be careful, however, using this method to contact folks you don't know.

There are oodles of rules you have to follow to avoid being listed as a spammer, particularly with those you do not already have a relationship with. It can be very costly to be charged with spamming. If you plan to use this method to contact people you don't know, be sure to study all the current laws and regulations, which we cannot go into here.

Don sets a lot of sales calls out of town, and he has a large list of contacts in each area. He has found email is a useful tool to contact a large number of current customers and prospects quickly and easily. It can be more productive than telephoning many prospects to set appointments.

Anywhere from a week to a day before Don heads off to a city, he sends out this email to those he would like to meet with:

> Hi <PROSPECT>,
>
> I'll be in your area <DAY, DATE> through <DAY, DATE>. If you have an upcoming project that will need custom-fabricated stainless-steel products, please let me know, and I'll arrange my schedule so we can meet at a time convenient to you. If you wish

to meet, you can respond to this email with a couple of convenient times or call / text my cell phone: 123-456-7890.

I send out these email notices to let folks know when I'll be in their area. This avoids the embarrassing situation of learning shortly after I return to my office that you have a need to meet with someone from <MY COMPANY>.

If you would prefer not to receive these emails, please tell me, and I'll promptly remove you from the notice list.

Regards,

Don Crawford, PE
<MY COMPANY>
(FULL ADDRESS)
(PHONE)
(FAX)
(EMAIL)

This technique works well because: It lets a large number of folks know you care about them, it tells them you also respect their time, and it keeps your name top of mind.

Don usually gets two types of responses:

1. "We don't have anything at this time. Thanks for letting me know when you'll be in the area." (These are the Expressives and Supportives. The Drivers and Analyticals simply delete the email if they don't have a need.)

2. Or "Yes, let's meet on Thursday morning. Call me to set a time."

For Don's most important contacts, Don also phones them to set appointments.

When telephoning someone you know, the process is similar, and the goal is the same as when you are phoning someone you don't know yet.

When there is a long selling cycle, with many on the decision-making team, you need to summarize the conversations to date and make sure nothing has changed.

Prospect: "Hello, this is Buddy."

Salesperson: "Hi, Buddy, this is Rachel. How are you doing today?"

Prospect: "Good, Rachel. How about you? I hope you are better than the last time we talked."

Salesperson: "Yes, thanks, my cold only lasted a few days. Do you have a few minutes or is this a busy time?"

Prospect: "I can talk now."

Salesperson: "Buddy, the last time we met you were going to gather some additional performance statistics for me. Do you have those?"

Prospect: "Yes, I got them a couple of days ago."

Salesperson: "Are they what you expected?"

Prospect: "Yes, some are even worse."

Salesperson: "It sounds like it's time to meet again to take a look at them. Would you have time tomorrow afternoon?"

Prospect: "Let's see. Tomorrow. I have time at either 11 a.m. or at 4:30 p.m. There is a meeting from 1 to 4."

Salesperson: "Hmm, let's see. I think 11 a.m. is good for me. Perhaps we could meet at your office for a half hour then go to an early lunch. You'd be back in plenty of time for your 1 p.m. meeting."

Prospect: "Sounds like a plan."

Salesperson: "Okay, we'll look at the statistics and see the implications of having your current productivity level."

Prospect: "Good enough, I'll see you tomorrow. Goodbye."

Summarizing the conversation helps you make sure everyone is singing from the same score. Now you're ready for the actual sales call, discussed in the next chapter (as soon as you finish your next challenges, of course).

Challenge Yourself

1. Look over your calendar for the past week. How many appointments did you have? How many of these were merely good and how many were outstanding? (Use your own scale to determine which was which.)

2. How many outstanding appointments do you need each week to meet your sales goals?

3. How successful were you in not selling when you were setting appointments?

CHAPTER SIXTEEN

Making the Sales Call

Now that you have an appointment, it's time to prepare for the sales call. A sales call is an event where the salesperson interacts with a purchaser.

Whenever you have an interaction with another person or persons for the ultimate purpose of convincing them to purchase your product or service, it's a sales call.

Sales calls can take place face-to-face or over the phone. Sales calls happen in the customer's office, in your store/office, or at neutral location. You can meet for a meal or on a golf course.

To be clear, however, sitting together with your best customer in Tuesday night Bible study is not a sales call. Nor is a casual meeting when picking your kids up from day care (although both build and maintain the relationship).

Plan Your Call

Whether you're meeting for a first time with a new unqualified prospect (suspect) or with one of your most valuable, long-time customers, always plan your sales call. Even if your selling is all done by telephone, it is equally important to plan the sales call.

The first step is pre-call planning. Don uses a pre-call sales call plan form which is a template in his ACT! contact-management software. Feel free to use the form below or revise it and make your own.

SALES CALL PLAN

DATE AND TIME OF MEETING:

CONTACT:

Address: ____________________

Address: ____________________

Phone: ____________________

Mobile Phone: ____________________

Alternate Phone: ____________________

GOAL:

POINT IN THE SELLING PROCESS:

TAKE:

LEAVE:

ASK ABOUT:

NOTES:

TO DO:

The top section of the pre-call planning sheet contains the basic information from the contact record, which is automatically updated by the software, along with the date and time of the meeting.

The second section identifies why you are investing your time in making this sales call:

1. What do you want to accomplish—the goal.

2. Where are you in the selling process: rapport, pain, budget, decision-making, presentation or post-sale activity?

3. What do you need to remember to take to the meeting?
    - Business card
    - Samples
    - PowerPoint presentation
    - Proposal
    - Promotional items, etc.

4. What do you plan to leave with the prospect or customer?

The "ask about" section helps you to organize your thoughts and make sure you take care of your agenda items.

For a first meeting, when building rapport is your goal, you might note to determine personality type. Don makes a doodle of a horizontal and a vertical line crossed at their midpoints. Once he has a sense of the prospect's personality type, he makes a mark in the appropriate quadrant (see Chapter 9 to learn more about personality types).

Then, note general rapport questions to fall back on if you get nervous or stuck with an Analytical or Driver who likes to give one-word answers. You might write down a technique you need to incorporate into your selling, like “use reversing” or “remember to clarify.” When you have completed these sections, you know why you are making the call and what you need to accomplish to make it pay off for you.

If you are in a one-call-close business, your goal is to make the sale. You’ll need to take with you whatever is necessary to finalize a sale.

If you sell carpet, then in your vehicle should be all the samples of the products you sell. Once you have a qualified prospect, then you can go to the car and get only the samples you need to make the sale.

Managing the Team

In team selling, you’ll need to designate a leader who determines who speaks when. The primary conversation needs to be between the leader of the selling team and the buying team’s decision maker.

Usually the senior member of each team takes the lead. When you are all peers, then assert your position as sales champion and take control of the meeting if it’s appropriate. Supporting members offer technical answers and clarifying questions. One member should be designated as the primary scribe and everyone should take their own notes, too. It’s the leader’s role to keep the selling team involved in the process.

Don’t let the discussion between the engineers in the room, for example, devolve into “free consulting;” that is, don’t give away too much information for free. Some prospects will do everything they can to pick your brain for free; if you give too much information to them, it will be harder to sell it later. They may just take your information and use it with another consultant. Not everyone is ethical.

If you are a member—or more importantly the leader—of a selling team, it's critical to have all members understand the plan. If they don't understand the plan, it would be like Chicago Bears going into a football game without practicing or using a playbook. Get your team together with sufficient time to rehearse how you want the sales call to go. Every member of the team needs to know their role.

As more technology is used, many meetings will be held by teleconference or web conference between two or more locations. It makes little difference whether it's video or audio conferencing, the team must still be rehearsed, and you need to clearly define roles. If the leader loses control in the teleconference, it will quickly degenerate to noise as all try to speak at once. Team members should take their cues from the leader.

Prospect Leader (Herman): "Beth, our manufacturing engineers don't understand why you need to know the average temperature in the plant."

Sales Leader (Beth): "Herman, I have Shannon Zellich, our software designer, here. Shannon, would you tell us why ambient temperature is important?"

Now Shannon has the floor (so to speak) and she answers Herman's concern. Meanwhile, Beth monitors the conversation to make sure it stays on track. When Shannon has finished, Beth takes over again.

Sales Leader: "Herman, does Shannon's explanation answer your question?"

Prospect Leader: "Yes, we understand now. Thank you."

This conversation can happen in person or by teleconference.

You have your appointment and your sales-call plan. There are a few more things to consider.

Decide What to Wear

Many books are written about dressing for success. We suggest you read several of them. The simplest rule of all is to dress like your customer dresses.

If you are calling on plant maintenance staff, you should anticipate going out to look at a problem in the plant. A nice business suit and spiked heels won't cut it here. You'll need comfortable trousers, shirt, and closed-toed shoes with low heels. Chances are you may need personal protective safety equipment as well: hard hat, hearing protection, safety glasses, and work gloves. If you have never been to a facility before, ask up front what the appropriate dress is.

If you have a presentation to the C-level staff—chief executive officers, chief information officers, chief operating officers, chief financial officers, and the like—of a corporation, the same rule applies: ask what the usual dress is. In the "old days," we all wore suits and men wore ties, but today it's common to find even the senior managers in business casual. The rule of thumb is to be comfortable yourself and to not make the prospect uncomfortable.

Use the Sales Process

If this is the first call, start at step one: building rapport, and don't move on until there is some "bonding." Then move through the process step by step.

If this is one of many calls you have had in a long selling cycle, start with rapport to continue the bonding process. Confirm previous discussions to be sure nothing has changed before moving on to the next step. Make sure you are on the same page and understand what your prospect is saying.

Here's an example from our friend Jeremy Vogan, a real estate sales representative, about clarifying what is said:

Jeremy (Salesperson): Early in my sales career I got a call from my sales assistant with an appointment she had lined up with a condo prospect. I met the prospect and showed her the home. I explained all the features and found out everything I could about her situation—or did I? After a couple of trial closes, I started getting the sense the prospect was ready to commit. Thinking she was interested in renting the condo, I asked her if she was interested in the home.

Prospect: "Well, I don't know, what is the price?"

Jeremy, smiling: "$1,240 per month. I have a simple one-page lease here . . ."

Prospect, frowning: "No, what is the ***price***?"

Jeremy: "I'm not sure what you're asking. $1,240 is the lease rate and it is also the amount of your security deposit."

Prospect: "Listen to me, young man. I never rent anything. What is the price if I am buying?"

Jeremy: "Uh, well, $190,000. We offer some great financing programs, but you would have to be prequalified..."

Prospect: "Nor do I ever finance anything. How do I buy this condo today?"

Jeremy: "We are on the same page now. I have a simple one-page ***purchase*** contract in my briefcase, and with a deposit of $2,500 we will sit down right here and write a cash contract to close in a week. Will that work for you?"

Prospect, beaming: "Yes! Let me get my checkbook."

As the above example shows, sometimes the best thing you can do is actively listen to your customer. Ask good questions and listen to the answers. When you actively listen to your customers, your customers know that you heard them and understood what they were saying. Active listening involves using different words to reflect or summarize what your customer said to you. Get it right, and you can start writing a contract.

Champion salespeople are world-class listeners. They use active listening skills to understand the customer's wants and needs. These skills can demonstrate empathy for the customer in their situation. A good salesperson will spend at least twice as much time listening as speaking. In fact, we recommend 70 percent listening and 30 percent speaking.

Reversing is the technique to use to keep the prospect talking. We discussed this in Chapter 9.

What to Do in the Lobby

You've arrived at your appointment a few minutes early and checked in with the receptionist. She announced you to your prospect, and asked you to have a seat in the lobby. Here are some tips on what to do while waiting.

- Mentally rehearse your opening statement.
- Look around at the pictures, samples, trophies and plaques on the wall. These will give you something to talk about to build rapport.
- Check out their catalogs to get an understanding of their business.
- Look at the magazines found in the lobby. What do they tell you about the company?
- If there are others waiting, introduce yourself. They might have insights to share about your prospect or the company. They likely sell to the same types of companies you do, so you can probably share leads. Or they might be your competition pitching business to the same prospect as you.

Learning About Your Prospect

Again, pay attention to what you see in the prospect's office. The artwork and personal items in the office reveal a good deal about your prospect.

Don't miss an opportunity to build rapport with your prospect by ignoring these items. If there is a fish on the wall, or a photo of a sailboat, comment on it. "I'll bet there's quite a story about that fish" is a good way to broach the subject. Your prospect will likely tell you an enthusiastic story.

Summary and Next Steps

During the sales call, write down your commitments to the prospect and his to you in the "To Do" section of your sales-call planning sheet. This will form the basis of the plan for the next sales call and for any necessary follow-up activities.

And don't forget: At the end of the call, schedule the next meeting and set the agenda.

Evaluating the Call

After you leave the sales call, do a "postmortem;" that is, evaluate the call. Turn the sales-call plan over and write down a list of all the things you did well.

- Did you achieve your goal for this call?
- Is their pain real?
- Does the budget match the problem?
- Did you find out how decisions to purchase your product or service are made?
- Did you get the order?
- What techniques did you use?

Then list the one or two things you need to improve. You can do this for the selling team as well as for yourself.

When you get back to your office or your car, do the follow-up tasks you committed to doing, such as having someone send literature, sending a request for proposal, etc.

Enter your sales-call notes into your contact-management software, adding the follow-up phone call or meeting to your calendar and task list. Take advantage of any automation features, such as reminders or recurring appointments.

Challenge Yourself

1. Evaluate your effectiveness for each sales call over the next month.

2. Use the Sales Call Planning Form (found in the appendix) for each sales call over the next month.

3. Keep track of what you learn when waiting in the lobby—note everything you learn about your prospect, the company, and additional potential customers, what problems they may have and other useful information.

4. Try different techniques for building rapport on the first sales call over the next month. Evaluate what works well and what doesn't.

5. Check your sales call follow-up performance. Did you meet all your prospects' expectations? How did this success move the sales process along?

CHAPTER SEVENTEEN

Cold Calling

Cold calls are a special kind of sales calls—those made without an appointment. A long time ago when communication technology wasn't as omnipresent as it is today, cold calls were the primary way to conduct a sales call. You could show up unannounced, and the prospect would usually see you. It's not the same today, but cold calls still have value.

What if you show up for your 10 a.m. meeting and find out the prospect was called out of town without notice? Rats! What do you do to productively fill the next hour?

Don always has a list of prospects with him he would like to meet someday. When the "A Team" is not available, he seeks an alternative.

The cold call is useful for information gathering. Receptionists are usually friendly and happy to help. Visit with the receptionist to find out who the appropriate person to talk with at a company is.

In large businesses the purchasing department typically has a policy not to see salespeople without an appointment. But buyers are human. Sometimes they are bored with the task they are doing and would like a diversion. Perhaps they are walking by on their way to the coffee machine. Maybe they have recently had a bad experience with your competitor and are looking for a new vendor. So you might get lucky and they will see you without an appointment. Ask to meet with them and see what happens.

Don has made lots of cold calls. In his experience, about half of the time he gets to talk with someone other than the receptionist. The other half of the time the receptionist will provide him with good information. So in our opinion, although it might be a bit scary or uncomfortable for you, a cold call is generally useful. Here's an example.

Despite a "No Soliciting" sign in the window of a hair salon, real estate sales representative Jeremy Vogan decided to do some information-gathering in the salon. He walked inside with some of his townhouse brochures and greeted the proprietor, a cheerful man from upstate New York. Jeremy asked if it was considered soliciting to tell him about his homes for sale.

The proprietor thought a moment and said, "Hm. Do you want me to actually buy one?"

"Well, yes!" Jeremy responded.

"Then it's probably soliciting!" he laughed. "It's okay, tell me what you've got." They talked for a while about his hair salon business and the local economy, and he owner took a handful of brochures and some business cards.

The next week the salon owner sent one of his best customers over to Jeremy and they were his very first cash townhouse buyer. They also ended up purchasing a second home from him later on. Needless to say, Jeremy has enjoyed a great relationship with the hair salon proprietor ever since.

"Be pleasant and give it a try," says Vogan. "If the salon owner would have jumped my case for coming into his store with sales materials, I would have bowed out graciously, but it's amazing what a smile and a conversation can bring."

Getting Past the Gatekeeper

Ever made repeated calls trying to reach a decision maker only to be rebuffed by the gatekeeper or voice mail? Then gather up your courage and make a cold call—but plan this one carefully. Start with the usual sales call plan because once you get face-to-face with the prospect, you're going to have to perform at your peak.

To get past the gatekeeper and talk to your prospect, you'll need a gimmick. Do some research about the target of your sales call. Perhaps you find out that your prospect loves the Green Bay Packers. Bring a Packers' hat or water bottle to give to them and let the gatekeeper know you want to give it to your prospect personally.

With a gift in your hand, the gatekeeper will be more inclined to call your prospect and let them know you are there.

It always works better, however, if your prospect has a sense of humor. It allows you to do something a little more outrageous.

Here are a few ideas:

- Bring a toy to make the gatekeeper smile, such as a pair of toy kissing ducks. You can say it represents what your customers want to do to you after they buy from you because they are so happy with your products.

- Bring in a birthday cake with lots of flaming candles. It doesn't make any difference whether it is the prospect's birthday or not. You want to create a memorable experience.
- Catch a ride on the same elevator and start a casual conversation: "Excuse me, aren't you (NAME)? Well this is my lucky day! I'm Katrina with the wind energy company. I've been wanting to talk with you. Now is probably not the appropriate time. So here's my card. When would be the best time to call and schedule an appointment? ... Would you introduce me to your assistant so when I phone her she will remember me?"
- Watch the video ***Pursuit of Happyness*** with Will Smith. See how he takes risks to reach his dream.
- Leave a small gift or promotional product related to the season, an upcoming holiday, or something that can remind them of your company.
- Bring food. It's easier to get a smile and an introduction when you have something good to share.

Perhaps you're now shaking your head saying, "This is stupid."

Well, maybe. It's a big risk. You don't use the gimmick technique unless the reward is worth it. Before trying these ideas, do your research to make sure this is the only way to get to the decision maker responsible for placing that million-dollar order.

Professional salespeople will try conventional selling techniques first. If traditional selling activities haven't worked, and you're convinced you can create pain and offer the right solution to improve the prospect's business or life, it's time to take the risk of looking foolish. Go for it.

Once you have a successful cold call experience, you will have the courage to try it again and again. Because now you know it can pay off!

Challenge Yourself

1. How do you feel about cold calls?

2. When your schedule unexpectedly opens up, how do you fill the time?

3. What creative ideas do you have for getting to the decision maker to make the deal of your lifetime?

4. If you are timid about making cold calls, list three things you can do to increase your confidence.

CHAPTER EIGHTEEN

Setting Your Goals

Goals help you plan your future. Goal setting is more than simply thinking about what you want to have next year. (That would be a wish or a hope, and hope is not a strategy.)

Goals give direction. Your goals should drive your life.

Too many average salespeople roll out of bed in the morning without having thought about what they need to accomplish for the day in order to be successful. When they get to the end of the driveway, they decide who they will call on, choosing which way to turn. Will they turn right and visit prospect No. 1, left to go to the office to make cold calls, or straight ahead to the coffee shop to check out the new barista?

Obviously, goal setting on the fly, so to speak, deciding at the end of the driveway which way to turn, would not help a sales representative become super successful. Unless you suddenly have a change in your schedule, making a spur-of-the-moment decision about what to do with your time is unproductive. Plan your activities and sales calls. Start with setting reasonable goals.

Write Down Your Goals

There are studies showing people who have written goals are more likely to realize them than those who don't. One sales trainer we know insists you are 1,000 times more likely to achieve your goals if you write them down. We're not sure if he has proven these statistics, but we have found that written goals—especially if they are written in the present tense—come to life much more quickly for us. For example, "I am the top-ranking salesperson in my company;" "I earn six figures annually in commissions;" or "I sell my paintings in the top ten galleries in New York City."

We recommend you write your goals in the present tense. Write goals for your attitude, your activities and your knowledge, as well as your life goals. Writing down both short-term and long-term goals will help you become more successful.

Selling, a Numbers Game

Successful salespeople do the same activities over and over. The more skill they have, the higher their success rate, but even poor selling done often enough can result in good sales numbers.

When you set your activities goals—or the things you must do daily to accomplish your goals—only set goals for what you can control. There is no point setting goals that require others to do something for you to achieve your goals. You can't control other people's behaviors.

The following example will show you how to set daily activity goals. All the numbers are made up, simply to show you how to set your activity goals.

The number of activities you might need to do as an auto salesperson would be different than what you need to do to sell multi-million-dollar construction equipment. Therefore, your numbers will vary from the examples.

Example 1 Assumptions:

- Closing ratio is one-third
- Average number of calls to get to the presentation step is 8
- Number of times to dial the phone to get an appointment is 10
- Average order is $10,000
- Annual sales goal is $1,000,000
- 250 work days a year

This means:

- Number of orders needed to reach the annual sales goals is: $1,000,000 (annual sales goal) ÷ $10,000 (average order) = 100
- Number of presentations is: 100 ÷ .33 (closing ratio) = 303
- Number of sales calls is: 303 x 8 = 2,424
- Number of times to dial the phone to get the 2,424 appointments is: 2,424 x 10 = 24,240
- Average number of dials per day is: 24,240 ÷ 250 = 97

Example 2 Assumptions:

- Closing ratio is one-half
- Average number of sales calls to get to the presentation step is 3
- Number of times to dial the phone to get an appointment is 20
- Average order is $2,500
- Annual sales goal is $300,000
- 250 work days a year

This means:

- Number of orders needed to reach the annual sales goals is: $300,000 (annual sales goal) ÷ $2,500 (average order) = 120
- Number of presentations is: 120 ÷ .50 (closing ratio) = 240
- Number of sales calls is: 240 x 3 = 720
- Number of times to dial the phone to get the 720 appointments is: 720 x 20 = 14,400
- Average number of dials per day is: 14,400 ÷ 250 = 58

The one thing you have total control over is the number of times you dial the phone. You can't control whether the prospect will answer or when they will have time to meet with you. So set the number of times you dial the phone each day and the law of averages says you'll meet your goal.

If you improve your performance, then the number of presentations will go down, your closing ratio will go up and you can either work less to get the same result or keep up the same level of activity and get better results.

The way to improve is to measure your activities. Don uses the form below (Phone Call Tracking Sheet) to track his "Dialing for Dollars" (what he calls telephoning prospects) activities. (The form is also found in Appendix 1.)

DAILY PHONE CALL TRACKING SHEET
FOR FOCUSED PHONING

NAME:______________________ DATE:__________

GOALS: (per 1-1/2 hours) DIALS_____ CONTACTS_____ APPOINTMENTS_____

RESULTS: _____ _____ _____

BEGINNING TIME: _____

										TIME
1	2	3	4	5	6	7	8	9	10	_____
11	12	13	14	15	16	17	18	19	20	_____
21	22	23	24	25	26	27	28	29	30	_____
31	32	33	34	35	36	37	38	39	40	_____
41	42	43	44	45	46	47	48	49	50	_____
51	52	53	54	55	56	57	58	59	60	_____
61	62	63	64	65	66	67	68	69	70	_____

ENDING TIME: _____

Prepared by:
Marketing Idea Shop, LLC
www.marketingideashop.com
www.softersideofselling.com

Each day, first thing in the morning or last thing at night, fill out your goals for the dials, contacts and appointments. When you begin calling, note your starting time on the form.

Every time you dial the phone, put a slash through the number (/ or half of an X). When you speak with the person you phoned, complete the X. When you actually schedule an appointment, circle the number with the X.

DAILY PHONE CALL TRACKING SHEET
FOR FOCUSED PHONING

NAME: Don DATE: 8/29/17

GOALS: (per 1-1/2 hours) DIALS 40 CONTACTS 10 APPOINTMENTS 4

RESULTS: 40 11 5

BEGINNING TIME: 8 AM

										TIME
1	2	3	4	5	6	7	8	9	10	820
11	12	13	14	15	16	17	18	19	20	830
21	22	23	24	25	26	27	28	29	30	855
31	32	33	34	35	36	37	38	39	40	915
41	42	43	44	45	46	47	48	49	50	
51	52	53	54	55	56	57	58	59	60	
61	62	63	64	65	66	67	68	69	70	

ENDING TIME: 915

Prepared by:
Marketing Idea Shop, LLC
www.marketingideashop.com
www.softersideofselling.com

Using this simple method, you track the number of times you dialed the phone and your success rate. You can also use it to determine the best time to make prospecting calls.

Keep Your Goal Prominent

Our daughter Erin was on the track team in high school. Being highly competitive, she liked to win the events she ran. And being quite bright, she knew what the winning times had to be.

Erin wrote her goal for the race on her hand in ink and this simple step kept it top-of-mind not only during her practice and race days, but all the time.

Erin trained hard and ate well to put herself in the position to win, but she also realized that winning is a mindset. And she succeeded. Erin set a school record and placed sixth in the State of Wisconsin in the low-hurdles event in 1995. Her record stood as the school's best until 2007, and today she remains in the school's top five winners. (Go Erin!)

This experience and others continue to help Erin win at everything she does. When she was a rising college senior, Erin was determined to get a good summer job that would not only give her excellent experience but also pay a good salary. She sat down with a local business directory and cold called business after business to find a summer job.

She also stood up at a golf outing of the local Sales and Marketing Executives International organization and said, "Can I have your attention? I'm Erin. I'm a rising senior at the University of Iowa studying biomedical engineering, and I need a summer job. If you have a job or know of someone who is looking for a smart, hard-working, dynamic summer employee, please come talk to me!"

Five or six people immediately sought her out, and she had a job in a week. Plus, she secured an internship at NASA's Langley Research Center and beefed up her resume.

So it goes to show you, if you think you're a winner, you will be, but you have to make a commitment to success.

Reaching success is a three-step process:

1. Set your goal.
2. Figure out what it takes to reach the goal.
3. Commit yourself without distraction to achievement of the goal.

Use the Telephone Tracking Sheet to monitor your appointment-setting effectiveness each week over the next month. What can you do differently to improve your sales appointment-setting proficiency?

Challenge Yourself

1. Improve your success now by filling in the blanks on the Goal Sheet below and then add some more of your own.

GOAL SHEET
(Insert your name in the first blank of each line.)

I __________ earn $________ per year.
I __________ am the No. 1 performer.
I __________ live in the ________________ neighborhood.
I __________ drive a ________________ (type of vehicle).

To reach these goals I do these activities:

I __________ make ________ prospecting calls a day.
I __________ meet with ________ prospects a week.
I __________ read ________ books about my business or industry a month.
I __________ know all about ________ industry.

CHAPTER NINETEEN

Getting & Staying Organized

The better you are at applying the sales process and techniques, the more efficient you'll be. The most successful salespeople are highly organized. If it's not their nature to be organized, they hire someone or find tools to help keep them on task.

Calendar

You'll need a calendar—only one. It should include everything you want to do and when you want to do it. One calendar, whether electronic or paper, will quickly show you where you need to be when. It will have time for appointments, sales management tasks, sales activities, visits to the gym, vacations, birthdays, anniversaries, and playtime all in one place. When two things need to happen simultaneously, you can quickly see the conflict and decide which takes precedence and what needs to be rescheduled.

Our daughter Abbi, who is a busy mother of three and a Disney World vacation planner with many clients, prefers a paper calendar to keep track of her obligations. She uses a planner with daily, weekly and monthly sheets. The daily sheets allow scheduling "to do" items on particular days, eliminating the overwhelming master "to do" list. But the paper system is not automatic. Abbi has to write the information down more than once.

However, she loves the ability to visually see all her appointments and activities. Carrying a paper planner can be a bit of a hassle because it's one more thing to carry, but it is easy to see if you are available for an appointment when your prospect proposes a date and time.

Don uses the calendar in his ACT! contact-management software. It's a complex system that automatically puts scheduled meetings on the monthly calendar and his daily reminder lists.

Lois prefers the Google electronic calendar that allows color coding of appointments and activities and integrates with all her devices. She gets reminders and alerts electronically on her phone, iPad and computer for each item.

One of the features in Google's calendar system is the ability to share the electronic calendar. You might want to look at Google Calendar if you need to keep others informed of your activities. Of course, the problem with an electronic system is you must be connected to update it (but you can print it and carry your paper copy).

Some companies have a company-wide calendar system, such as Microsoft Outlook, Microsoft Meeting or another similar product. With a tool like this, you can quickly see when all necessary parties are available, and you can electronically schedule the meetings.

The point is, use whatever calendar works best for you,

but use only one calendar to schedule your whole life. Synchronize it periodically with your business associates and family to make sure your calendar is up-to-date.

Organize Your Office

The time-management gurus tell us we waste lots of time looking for stuff we need because it's not organized properly. They also advise us to handle a piece of paper or electronic mail only once. If you immediately place your documents in the proper place, you will always know where to find them, and you'll avoid a messy office.

Don's desk is always clean and organized, but he likes to keep everything because it might be needed someday. For him, the computer has been a blessing, especially since there are such terrific tools to search for files on the computer these days.

Lois has a messy office. When she is very busy, she doesn't take time to put things away and it creates more chaos for her. Every once in a while, she has to stop what she's doing and clean her office. It's a big waste of time, and she knows it, but she is often working on several projects at the same time and her office gets messy. The messier her office is, the harder it is for her to work.

She would greatly benefit by having an administrative assistant clean up after her every day! But since she doesn't have an assistant, she has devised ways to stay organized, such as writing in her Google calendar, sending herself emails summarizing conversations and things needing completion, using a to-do list, keeping folders for each project where she puts all the items related to the project so it's easier to find things, and organizing her "piles" by tasks (bills, client projects, reading material, etc.). When she takes the time at the end of the day to clean off her desk and update her to-do lists, she accomplishes more the next day.

Right now go through your office (Lois too!)—your desk, shelves, drawers, file cabinets—and toss out everything you'll probably never need again. Then think about how you work. Organize the remaining files and materials around your style. Is your life task-driven? Are you event-driven? Do the demands of prospects and customers drive your activities?

Put the items you need often in a convenient location. Reference material can be cataloged and stored in a logical way for you. Better yet, find someone else who is better at keeping up with stuff you occasionally use and let them be a resource for you. Clear off your desk except for what you need for the task at hand.

Things That Inspire You

Your office doesn't have to be minimalistic. Decorate it with family pictures, art, and items to make it a pleasant place to work. Use a bulletin board or similar item to post inspirational quotes, phone scripts, notes and calendars where you can easily see them when the phone rings and you need the information. Keep your goals posted somewhere within your line of sight. It will help your brain surreptitiously work toward your goals.

Don has two shelves of toys—some are practical but most are silly things. When he is having a creative block, a few minutes trying to make the yo-yo work or fiddling with a stress ball often jump starts his creativity. The most important feature in Don's office is the photo of Lois. It's a constant reminder of why he works to be successful.

Lois created a "treasure map" visually representing her goals, which are life goals, not simply business goals. It is a poster-size photo montage reflecting all her goals and sources of happiness. It is hung on the wall near her desk. She also has many pictures of her family surrounding her workspace because they are her main reason for working.

What keeps you going? Make sure you can see its representation easily when you are at your desk.

Your Mobile Office

How much time do you spend on the road in your car? Is it your mobile office?

Go to any department, office supply, or hardware store and you'll find a cornucopia of bins and totes to keep the stuff you need for your sales calls organized. Where's your box of business cards? Back at the office or in your car? Don keeps his in the car and a small stack in the office.

Don has six folders: one for each weekday and one marked "next week." He puts everything he needs for sales calls into the folder for the specific day. As he plans his week, he moves the stuff from "next week" into the appropriate day.

He keeps two other folders as well: "follow up" and "prospects." In the follow-up folder are all the proposals and tasks that need to be watched closely either by contacting an associate in the office or the customer. The "prospect" folder has information on suspects (those who have not yet been qualified). When Don has a few spare minutes, he'll phone to qualify and set appointments with someone from the folder.

He keeps these folders in a plastic file box that fits handily in his car. In the trunk he has a hard hat, work boots, a safety vest and work gloves, which he needs when he visits prospects or customers on construction sites. There are totes with literature and promotional items. These get refilled after each trip to be sure there is always an ample supply. A charger for the mobile phone and a hands-free attachment to use while driving stay in his car all the time. Of course, new cars have Bluetooth connectivity now, so the hands-free device is not as critical. He also always carries a set of maps for wherever he is going, even though he can now use GPS and map applications on his phone. The paper maps are easy to view a larger area to see relative locations of clients.

Briefcase

What's in your briefcase? Carry only what's needed for your sales meeting or presentation. Don't carry things from past meetings with other clients; clean out your briefcase before you go to your sales appointment. Make sure you have business cards, a pad of paper, a working pen, and the documents, brochures, and other materials relative to this particular sales meeting. Get rid of everything else.

Remember, if you have a walking territory in a high-density area of a major city, you'll need to treat your brief case differently. You should tote with you everything needed for the sales calls until you return to your car or office.

If you carry a purse, we suggest you rid yourself of it and put whatever is absolutely needed from it in your briefcase. You will only have one item to carry, and won't fumble around with multiple bags.

Don't skimp on your briefcase; make sure it is easy to carry both over your shoulder and with handles, and it has plenty of space for your files and the few personal items you need.

Computer

Your computer (or other electronic device) is a valuable sales tool only if it is organized so you can find what you need quickly. Be sure you know how to easily locate errant files.

With ACT! contact manager, you can attach files, emails, pictures, etc., to each contact. When you look up a contact, all the relevant correspondence is there. Don keeps the business section of his computer organized in this manner (with each bullet being a computer folder):

- Calendar
- Competition
- Customers
- Forecast
- General
- Graphics
- Management
- Marketing
- Memberships
- Presentations
- Prospects
- Publicity
- Sales Meetings
- Sales Processes
- Sales Territory
- Standard Letters
- Suspects

In the "prospects" folder are individual folders for each active prospect. Likewise, the "customers" folder holds a folder for each customer. Don keeps all the documents for each in their respective folders. With about a gazillion bites of storage in his hard drive he rarely takes time to clean out these folders.

He uses an online back-up service to keep his data safe. Nearly all the information he needs to manage his customers and move the prospects through the process of becoming customers is found in his laptop. With a couple of key strokes, emails can be attached to a contact in ACT! or moved to the appropriate folder.

Lois organizes her computer files in a similar manner. Within each client folder, each type of document is coded so she knows exactly what it is. For instance, a letter (abbrieviated LT) written on June 1 to accompany a proposal for her client Supply House (client abbreviation SH) would be labeled something like: SHLTproposal_6-1-2017 and filed in the appropriate client's or prospect's folder.

Your organization method may be different than ours. The point is you should have a way to keep yourself organized, whether you use a phone application, a file system on your computer, or index cards. The method doesn't matter as long as it works for you and you use it religiously.

Keeping organized is a process. You need to schedule time each week to review your organization. We think the best technique to increase your efficiency is to concentrate on only one task at a time. However, when many things are happening simultaneously, you may need to be flexible.

Here are some ways to be more productive:

- Set your email program to only download email at your command.
- Turn off your Facebook alerts!

- Screen your calls or turn off the phone when you need the time to concentrate on the task at hand.
- Close your office door.
- Set a certain period of time to work on each project; if you schedule it, it will get done.
- Tackle your biggest problems or those needing the most creativity when you are at your best. The process will go much quicker than if you are tired.
- Clear away everything not related to the task at hand.
- Focus your attention on the most important task.
- Make a daily "To Do" list, and cross off items as you do them, rescheduling tasks to the future that do not get finished today.

If you follow these suggestions, you'll get your task done faster and be able to move on to the next one—getting more done in a day than you ever thought possible.

Challenge Yourself

1. Take an inventory of all the materials you use in your job.

2. For one week, measure how long it takes you to find what you need. Whether it's stored in a drawer, on your laptop or in a pile somewhere; list what you need, why you needed it and how long it took to locate it.

3. From the list you created, determine the effectiveness of your current system. If it takes you minimal time to find stuff, then you're okay. If your frustration level climbs with each task you need to do, then start fixing your system. If you need help developing a workable structure, hire an organizing specialist to create a system you can effectively use.

CHAPTER TWENTY

Sales Tools

When Don's dad was selling in the 1960s and 70s, his most valuable tools were his Rolodex® and calendar. Technology was a telephone and a manual Royal typewriter. After a sales call, since it was well before mobile phones had been invented, he'd borrow the customer's office phone to call in the order to his inside-sales guy. When he got home on Friday afternoons, he'd prepare his reports on the Royal typewriter and drop them in the mail.

Salespeople had fewer accounts; prospecting was a tedious process. And lead generation depended on the company's direct mail and print advertising campaigns for most B2B sales. In one sense, life was simpler then. Almost all of Don's father's success depended on building strong personal relationships with each of his customers.

Now we have the Internet, email, mobile phones, computers, GPS and tablets. How can all this technology improve your performance? Let's look at a few of the tools in our toolbox and how we use them.

Researching and Gathering Intelligence

With the Internet—Google and other search engines, Wikipedia, Facebook, LinkedIn and other social media, and online databases, etc.—information is almost instantly available. Of course, it's best to have multiple sources of the same information so you can be assured it's correct. And although Wikipedia can be helpful, you can't completely rely on it since anyone can add entries and they aren't verified.

Doing research before your all-important first meeting is invaluable. You won't waste your prospect's time with unnecessary questions. You'll be asking about their business from a position of strength based on what you have learned from your research. It will help you build rapport. And as we've said many times previously, we believe the first and perhaps most important step in the sales process is building rapport.

The two hazards of Internet research are quality of information and quantity of information.

You'll find many different articles, press releases and directory listings for each inquiry. The successful salesperson validates what was learned from the online search so as not to be embarrassed when discussing with the prospect what they ***thought*** was fact.

The vast quantity of information often leads to what one associate refers to as "getting lost in the weeds," or sidetracked by all the details. It'll take discipline not to be distracted from the primary research objective.

Begin each research project by writing down the question you want answered. Here's an example: Don's company has a few customers in Lynchburg and the company often runs its delivery trucks less than half full. This adds cost and reduces profits. When his company develops more customers, it will be more efficient and profits will rise because trucks will be filled with multiple deliveries that will be shipped at the same time.

Don wonders, “Are there other companies in the area or along the route from our plant to Lynchburg that would be good potential prospects?”

You can then structure your research to answer the question. This works whether you are a solopreneur or have a large corporate research department supporting your sales effort. From the example, you see the researcher knows why the question is important and specifically what data is needed.

One of the ways to research this is to set up Google Alerts. Not only can you find companies in Lynchburg, but you can also learn all about your hot prospects and current trends in your industry through this free service. You can even set them up for your own company or yourself. Google data mines the web and sends you daily or weekly emails for each alert you set up.

It’s also an extremely easy way to gather competitive information. You’ll know where your competitor is posting their information online, when your prospects have been mentioned in the newspaper, and a great deal of valuable information if you include the right search terms to gather this intelligence.

Communicating with Customers and Prospects

When used appropriately, email is a valuable tool, but it can also be a detriment. In the “old days” when prospecting, you’d often hear, “Send me some literature.” Then—as now—

this request is a conversation killer. The prospect is generally only trying to get you off the phone.

In the past, you'd have to write a note, gather some literature, put it in an envelope and take it to the post office. Then you'd wait several days to call again to see if the prospect received it. What a waste of time!

With email, you can customize your response for the prospect, send it in a matter of minutes, request a read receipt, and call back within an hour or a day at most. For more details on how Don uses email to set appointments, see Chapter 15.

Email can be used in the presentation step, but only under very controlled conditions. For small recurring business from a customer with whom you have a strong relationship, a simple price quotation may get you the order. If this is a new customer, however, you need to fight your way in to a personal presentation.

There will be times when only a written submittal will be allowed. The resulting proposal needs to have all the same elements of an in-person presentation: build rapport, restate the pain, confirm the budget, reiterate the decision-making process, present your solution and expertise and ask for the order.

With email you can include photos, charts, and links to websites to bolster your case. You can even combine a phone conversation with the electronic presentation to enhance it. Remember, with electronic submission you get no immediate feedback. The telephone or teleconference offers some vocal signals, but the best place to be for an important presentation is face-to-face with the prospect.

The telephone has long been a useful tool for the salesperson and now mobile phones have increased its effectiveness. Of course, cell phones have evolved into much more than simple voice communication tools. These devices are really powerful computers that fit in the palm of your hand.

Set all the special features of the portable electronic device aside for a minute and simply consider the voice communication feature of the cellular phone or the wired telephone (believe it or not, some people and businesses still have landlines—and, for your information, text communication doesn't work on them yet). For many years this has been and continues to be the primary tool of the successful salesperson.

The phone can be used to gather information, set appointments, get referrals, confirm meetings, coordinate activities among your peers, make reservations, and myriad other tasks. With mobile phones this can be done virtually anywhere, which is a benefit and a curse. The value is you are always available to your customers. The curse is you are always available to your customers. But remember, you can choose when to answer the phone. You do not necessarily have to be available 24/7 to be successful in sales.

Today, when we go to the movies or to a live performance, the pre-show announcements always include a reminder to turn off your cell phone. When you are meeting with a customer, the same applies. Turn off your cell phone and give the customer your uninterrupted attention.

If there is a need to have your cell phone on, such as your wife is pregnant and expecting to deliver soon, then at the beginning of the meeting, tell your prospect you may need to take a call. Or perhaps you need to get an answer to a question phoned to you during the meeting from your office staff. With today's cell phone technology, you can screen the calls and answer only the important ones. Your prospect has honored you with their time; respect their commitment.

Do More with Software

Every day we hear, "Gotta do more with less." We recommend finding technology options to save you time and effort. We have told you about several in this book, but by the time you read this, it's likely there will be many new options.

Contact-management software, such as the ACT! database program we mentioned earlier, will help you keep in touch with your customers. Contact-management software is an appropriate description for a computer tool that helps you keep track of your tasks and activities, prioritizes your prospects and customers and increases efficiency in communicating with them.

ACT! isn't the only product out there. Some large companies use proprietary systems to connect very large sales teams. Lois has effectively used Microsoft Outlook (part of the Office Suite). A small business might find Outlook is a great tool for them. If you don't have contact-management software, then do an Internet search and determine which product is right for you.

Nowadays, contact-management systems have applications that work with portable electronic devices and synchronize with the database on the server.

With some software, contacts can be grouped together by a variety of search criteria—location, type of industry, and company are the most common ones.

Besides contact information, contact-management software helps you keep track of the activities for each contact.

You can see when you last spoke or met and the content of the conversation. A calendar is automatically updated each time an activity is scheduled. Reports to track progress and history are a few keystrokes away. As we've noted previously, Don's software allows him to send emails to everyone in a city announcing his visit with a few key strokes. For successful salespeople today, a good contact-management software is essential.

On the other hand, like the Internet, contact-management software can be a time waster. To make it useful, you have to input the information. Most software programs are designed with features to serve various sizes of companies. Don has found you can waste a lot of time inputting data that's of little use in gaining new business. Decide which database fields and software features increase your effectiveness and ignore the others. From time to time, revisit the software's sales website to get ideas on how to improve your performance. Evaluate carefully each new feature added to determine whether it will increase your efficiency.

Written Communications

Sales letters are old tools, and they never go out of style. With contact-management software, sending a sales letter either by postal mail or email is simple. If you're an expert at Microsoft Outlook, you can also handle these tasks using this software. For instance, you can individually email your customers and prospects the same newsletter, with the software filling in the correct email address and salutation.

Remember, the content of the sales letter still needs to be compelling. The headline (or subject line) needs to grab attention, the body copy establishes pain and then presents a solution, and the letter closes with a call to action. Writing good sales letters is an art (and outside the scope of this book). If you are not expert at it, hire someone to do it for you or take time to study how to write good sales letters.

Simply writing and sending a sales letter is not sufficient. You have to follow up. For large campaigns, follow up might be multiple letters designed to pique interest and compel action. For smaller campaigns, a phone call is the ideal follow up. The successful salesperson uses sales letters to find new prospects and then contacts them to make an appointment—always following the system of building rapport, finding the pain, discovering the budget and determining the decision-making process before presenting their solution and asking for the order.

Your most important tool as a salesperson is taking notes during phone conversations and personal meetings. Whether you do it with pad and pen or electronically, notes are valuable in closing sales. When you take notes, it shows the prospect you are interested.

The benefit to you, particularly in long meetings, is to capture all the problems, their implications and payoff benefits. You can then attack them one at a time. It also provides a summary of what went on at the meeting. When you get back to your office, if you would like, you can scan the notes and send them to all interested parties as well as add them to the contact-manager software.

Use Forms and Checklists

Make your own form or checklist, or use the Sales Call Planning Form we discussed earlier in Chapter 16. You'll also find a copy of the Sales Call Planning Form in Appendix 1.

This form helps keep you on track, impresses your prospect with your organization skills and is a vehicle for saving information in long selling cycles.

We've found that it can be a real benefit to mix things up with contacts, i.e., visits, calls, messages, and in-person pop-ins. Even a funny email joke (or these days, a meme) can help you to stand out in the prospect's mind.

Challenge Yourself

1. List the top ten causes limiting your sales productivity.

2. For each limitation write the reason you think it is counter-productive and your estimation of how much your sales would improve if it were eliminated.

3. Brainstorm sales tools that would eliminate or minimize each limitation.

4. Research to find existing tools or create ones to help you be more productive.

CHAPTER TWENTY-ONE

Buying Signals

There are many books and videos about understanding and interpreting body language, but don't get too wrapped up in trying to learn all the nuances of these techniques.

By the time you have reached an age where you are selling professionally, you probably have learned and use nearly everything in those books. Don's mother always knew when he was lying; your mother probably did too. His mom never read those books, yet she could see it in his face and hear it in his voice. Trust your instincts, and you will probably do fine interpreting body language.

Don confesses he read one or two of those books long ago. He found he was so distracted trying to intentionally interpret all the signals that he missed most of them, along with the buying signals he normally quickly understands.

Lois, on the other hand, finds these methods enlightening. If you believe understanding body language is your weakness, by all means, study it. Just don't get so involved with looking for specific body movements you miss the buying signals. (We discussed some techniques in Chapter 9.)

You know in your gut when your prospect is ready to become your customer. They start talking about life after the sale. "When can you deliver the new boat?" "Can I pay for this with my credit card?" "Tell me how the warranty works." In team buying situations, the decision maker looks at the purchaser and says, "Felix, you take it from here."

When you recognize the decision maker is ready to commit, shut up. Stop your presentation. It has done what you needed it to do.

Say, "Thank you!" and move on to completing the paperwork.

Novice salespeople get so wrapped up in the presentation they go on presenting long after the prospect is convinced. In many cases they'll talk themselves right out of the order.

With the selling process we advocate, commitment often happens without a presentation. If the salesperson has identified the decision maker and prepared a solution that takes away the pain within the budget, then they move right to the commitment.

As we've said before, the key is to eliminate the option for the decision maker to think it over. Get your prospect to give a Yes (then you can celebrate) or a No (then you can go right on selling).

Challenge Yourself

1. Over the next month, concentrate on reading your prospects' nonverbal signals.

2. At the end of each sales call, write down what you "felt" about the sales call. Note how you "knew" what to say next.

3. Concentrate on not "presenting past the close," that is, stop talking after you get a "yes."

CHAPTER TWENTY-TWO

Customer Management

There are good customers, great customers and, well, let's face it—those you wish you'd never met. What distinguishes a good customer from a great one? It's the relationship.

Great customers like you, ***really*** like you. They appreciate the value you personally bring to their business and to their professional lives. Great customers have respect for you, and you have respect for them.

Will they—from time to time—place orders with your competition? Perhaps. When they do, they'll tell you why.

With great customers you have multiple relationships throughout the whole organization. Great customers rarely "bid out" projects (meaning ask other companies to provide a bid in addition to yours) you could do for them. And they always pay their bills on time.

Great customers have the capacity to purchase high volumes from you. Good customers have fewer needs.

Good customers have most of the traits of great ones, but you have not yet built the relationships between your company and theirs to the highest level. They are great customers in progress. Good customers buy selected products and services from you while great customers buy across all your product lines. They see value in what you offer.

Customer relationship management is the art of meeting and exceeding customer expectations. All businesses have limited resources and each salesperson only has a finite number of hours each day and each week.

It's amazing how the Pareto Principle (also known as the "80/20 rule") works in selling: 80 percent of your business comes from 20 percent of your customers. Those 20 percent are your great customers and where you will spend 80 percent of your time. The other 20 percent of your time is spent working on converting good customers to great ones.

With the great customers, you and your team are integral resources to their business. When they have a problem your team can solve, they will phone you or another member of your staff to solve the problem. Your primary job with great customers is post-sale activities, including:

- Keeping up with personnel changes at their company and continuing to keep them informed of changes at your company.
- Finding new prospects within the great customer's organization. You can do this either at locations where you currently do business or at other facilities where they are buying from your competitor.

As you create new, great customers, your sales territory increases and your compensation grows. Great customers take less time to manage per dollar of sales, freeing you to spend time moving good customers into the great category.

Don has many great customers in his territory. Most of the time they are trained to directly phone the project engineer who handles their account. Recently one of the project engineers at Don's company moved on to other employment. During the transition period, Don made sure all calls for help from the customer's team went to him. He handled the problems and introduced the new project engineer to the customer, monitored the relationship to be sure it was gelling and insured the long-lasting relationship would stand the possibility of sniping by competitors. Yes, this took time away from hunting new business, but it is an excellent investment in the mutually-beneficial, long-term relationship the two companies have experienced.

What Can You Do About Bad Customers?

Fire them! They will suck the life out of you, take energy away from serving the good and great customers and frustrate your entire customer-service organization.

It's unlikely that you will be able to train them to become good or great customers. These bad customers are best served by your competition.

When you fire a customer, do it professionally with a face-to-face meeting. It's never good to burn your bridges; bad customers can be like a bad penny and keep turning up in another situation. When you meet with this customer, explain why you believe the two companies are not compatible and get their feedback.

In some cases it's a mutual misunderstanding that can be cleared up and they can be converted to a good or great customer. In other cases, you'll agree there is no perceived value in the relationship and will agree to move on.

Of course, there are always other possibilities. Let us tell you what happened on one of Don's projects.

Don's company was working for the general contractor on a large pharmaceutical company's plant-modification project. The owner's project manager was—to put it delicately—hard to deal with. He would continually demand changes in the scope of the project and not issue change orders. He delayed in approving invoices for payment, and did other unprofessional actions that were uncooperative and infuriating.

The general contractor on the project had finally had enough. The contractor gave notice it intended to cancel the job, which got the attention of the pharmaceutical company's senior management. The contractor had kept good records and presented their case to the pharmaceutical company's management. The company's project manager was replaced with a more competent one and the project proceeded with a much smoother relationship to a successful conclusion.

Be respectful of your bad customers. Be creative. Do your best to solve the problems, be communicative, and take care of yourself and your company. If necessary, fire them.

Challenge Yourself

1. Think about what makes a great customer for you.

2. Evaluate each of your customers—rating them as great, good or bad.

3. Either "fire" the bad ones as quickly as you can, or convert them to good ones. How will you make these changes?

4. Create a strategy to convert each of your good customers to great ones.

5. Develop a system for evaluating your company's performance with each of your great customers. Persuade others in your company to help in maintaining and further developing great customers.

CHAPTER TWENTY-THREE

The Competition

Don has the best competitors in the world. They compete with integrity and do a credible job for their customers. When sales professionals do this, we jointly raise the level of business ethics for the industry.

Why should you even care about your competitors? As nice as they are, they are still out to take away your best customers. They, like you, are constantly growing and changing as a business, trying to keep one step ahead of you.

Pay attention to what they're doing. Check out their company website, read their literature, and talk to their customers to see what these customers like about them. Learn as much as you can about them—including the strengths and weaknesses of their salespeople—so you can defeat them in the game of commerce. When you know their strengths and weaknesses, you can position yourself and your business to take advantage of your strengths against their weaknesses.

Being Available When the Competitor is Not

If your competitor is a top-notch golfer and member of a popular country club and your prospect loves golf, you may be vulnerable in rapport building. Your goal is to figure out how to take this strength and portray it as a weakness, while still maintaining your integrity. Here's one way to approach it:

Salesperson: (searching for pain) "Has there ever been an occasion when you needed help from your current supplier and they weren't available?"

Prospect: "As a matter of fact, from time to time it's taken a day or two to hear back from them, especially when it's golf season because our current salesperson spends a lot of time on the golf course."

Salesperson: (creating pain) "How did that affect your business?"

Prospect: "It's frustrating not to be the most important person in the salesman's life. When we need attention, I expect to be taken care of."

Salesperson: (increasing the pain) "How often does it happen?"

Prospect: "In the summertime during golf season, it is more frequent. It seems like since we signed the multi-year contract with his company, our rep is not around as often."

Salesperson: "What do you do when you don't get the service you expect because he's on the golf course?"

Prospect: "Since we have a contract, I generally have to wait for him. What can I do?"

Salesperson: (looking for an opportunity) "Would you do me a favor? The next time you can't get in touch with your current supplier, would you give me a call?"

Prospect: "Okay, but remember we have this long-term contract so I can't promise anything."

Salesperson: "Fair enough. I want to help you succeed whenever I can. Perhaps the next time the contract is renewed, you will consider my company."

Integrity Wins

Don Miguel Ruis in his book ***The Four Agreements*** advises us to always be "impeccable with our word." Whatever we do in the great game of sales, we must do with integrity.

The first rule is to never speak ill of a competitor. In the conversation on the previous page the salesperson asked some low-key questions to get the prospect to draw his own conclusions about the competition.

As you move through your selling career, you'll meet those who will speak ill of you and your company. Don't stoop to their level. When asked by your prospects or customers to confirm rumors about your competition, it's a good time for a reverse.

Prospect: "Did you hear there is a family feud at brand X?"

Salesperson: "That's interesting. How do you think the family problems will affect your relationship with them?"

Competitive Research, Trade Shows and Collaboration

When you attend a trade show, it's a good time to learn about your competition. Here are our rules for engaging competitors at trade shows:

- Plan to visit with them when traffic is slow.
- If one of their customers or a prospect stops by their booth, excuse yourself. Don't hang around and eavesdrop.
- Take literature, price lists, sales premiums, etc., only if offered.
- Use the opportunity to find areas of potential collaboration as well as conflict. Determine what they do for their customers that your company can't or won't do.

Knowing your competition well allows you to better serve your customers. There may even be times when it is mutually beneficial for two competing companies to collaborate to serve a customer. No, we're not talking about collusion or price fixing or other illegal activities.

When Don was in the fire-protection business, competitors who had territories contiguous to his company's would often snipe at accounts in the border areas. And Don did the same.

This was good healthy competition and the customers benefited from having choices for solutions.

When large projects came along—too big for either company to take on alone—the companies would jointly pitch the work. By working collaboratively, both companies were able to get some of the business and serve the customer well.

There are also times when it's to your benefit to refer a customer to a competitor. When the cost of serving the customer exceeds the benefit you derive from their business, it's time for someone else to provide those services. Perhaps another company could profitably serve them.

Other times it's a benefit to your customer to pass them off to a competitor. (What? Lose sales by intentionally getting my competitor in the door? Maybe.) Remember, our goal is to develop mutually-beneficial, long-term relationships with our best customers.

Successful salespeople get there by paying attention to the needs of the customer over their own. When your customer has a problem your company can't solve, it's time to refer them elsewhere. It could be a short-term capacity limitation causing you to refer your customer elsewhere; it could be a quality issue you're not equipped to deal with; or it may require an investment your company is not willing to make.

For this one issue you can bring in a competitor. "High risk!" you might think. Perhaps, but not if you do it well.

First, have the discussion with your customer and explain why your company can't meet their needs at this time. If changes are being made so eventually you can provide the product or service, tell them about these changes.

Then explain how important it is to you that they have their needs met.

Next, schedule an appointment to bring in your competitor to meet with the customer. Quite frankly, your competitor is going to find a way to meet the needs on which you can't deliver anyway. You might as well be the catalyst and get the points from your customer and the competitor for doing it. (And, of course, you will be sure to choose a competitor who displays integrity.)

Challenge Yourself

1. How well do you understand your competitor's strategies? Write a list of all your competitors, their strengths and weaknesses. Then contrast your strengths against their weaknesses from the customers' point of view.

2. How can you collaborate with your competitors to add value to your customer's business?

3. Are you active in trade associations where you can meet and get to know your competitors?

4. How do you handle situations where you find yourself and a competitor with a customer at the same time?

CHAPTER TWENTY-FOUR

Conclusion: Good Selling

> "Every day in Africa a gazelle wakes up. It knows it must run faster than the fastest lion or it will be killed. Every morning a lion wakes up. It knows that it must outrun the slowest gazelle or it will starve to death. It doesn't matter whether you are a lion or a gazelle. When the sun comes up, you better be running."
>
> ~Abe Gubegna
> Ethiopia, circa 1974

The world is filled with great salespeople. Each of them has learned to practice their craft with skill. They have internalized the system and techniques and used them until they are second nature. Nevertheless, these salespeople spend time each day perfecting their craft by reading and studying to build their skills faster than their competitors.

Plan your day, work your plan. Believe in yourself and you will be among the best of the best. Good selling!

Challenge Yourself

1. What will you do each day to improve your selling skills?

2. Create a scorecard for yourself. Grade every contact you have with a prospect or customer: What did you do well, what should you have done better, what will you do next time?

3. At the end of each week, review your scorecards and put together a personal development plan for the next week.

4. Get a mentor.

APPENDIX 1

Forms & Additional Resources

PERSONAL INVENTORY FORM

Strengths:

- _______________
- _______________
- _______________
- _______________
- _______________

Weaknesses:

- _______________
- _______________
- _______________
- _______________
- _______________

SALES SKILLS INVENTORY QUIZ

Rank yourself from 1 to 10 with 10 being the best and 1 being the worst on the following statements.

___ I am a good problem solver.
___ I keep my goals in mind and work toward them every day.
___ If someone says "No" to me, I never take it personally.
___ I keep a list of what I need to do and I cross the items off as I accomplish them.
___ I know how many sales I made last month/week/year.
___ I am a self-starter.
___ I successfully accomplish what I set out to do.
___ I am an optimistic person.
___ I am able to handle most stresses well.
___ I am motivated to win.
___ I like to meet new people.
___ I'm comfortable shaking someone's hand when we meet.
___ I can introduce myself without stumbling over my words.
___ When I ask people to do things, they generally comply.
___ People tell me they admire me.
___ I am organized and can keep myself on task.
___ I am reliable; when I say I will do something, I do it.
___ I am persistent; it takes a lot to make me give up.
___ I am intuitive and easily understand others.
___ I am a good listener.
___ I am honest and ethical.
___ I am happy.
___ I love helping others.
___ Talking to people is easy for me.
___ I am outgoing and cheerful.

How did you rank?

175-380: Excellent sales skills
100-174: Good sales skills
75-99: Study hard!
0-74: It might be time to look for another profession

SALES CALL PLAN

DATE AND TIME OF MEETING:

CONTACT:

Address: ____________________________

Address: ____________________________

Phone: _____________________________

Mobile Phone: ______________________

Alternate Phone: ____________________

GOAL:

POINT IN THE SELLING PROCESS:

TAKE:

LEAVE:

ASK ABOUT:

NOTES:

TO DO:

DAILY PHONE CALL TRACKING SHEET
FOR FOCUSED PHONING

NAME:______________________________ DATE:____________

GOALS: (per 1-1/2 hours) DIALS_____ CONTACTS_____ APPOINTMENTS_____

RESULTS: _____ _____ _____

BEGINNING TIME: __________

										TIME
1	2	3	4	5	6	7	8	9	10	________
11	12	13	14	15	16	17	18	19	20	________
21	22	23	24	25	26	27	28	29	30	________
31	32	33	34	35	36	37	38	39	40	________
41	42	43	44	45	46	47	48	49	50	________
51	52	53	54	55	56	57	58	59	60	________
61	62	63	64	65	66	67	68	69	70	________

ENDING TIME: __________

Prepared by:
Marketing Idea Shop, LLC
www.marketingideashop.com
www.softersideofselling.com

GOAL SHEET
(Insert your name in the first blank of each line.)

I ________ earn $ ________ per year.
I ________ am the No. 1 performer.
I ________ live in the ________ neighborhood.
I ________ drive a ________ (type of vehicle).

To reach these goals I do these activities:

I ________ make ________ prospecting calls a day.
I ________ meet with ________ prospects a week.
I ________ read ________ books about my business or industry a month.
I ________ know all about ________ industry.

APPENDIX 2

Definitions

4Ps: product, price, place, promotion

Ambition: a desire to achieve

Auditory people: people who learn primarily by hearing

B2B: business-to-business sales, that is, one business selling to another business

B2C: business-to-consumer sales, that is, a business selling to individuals rather than businesses

Benefits: the reasons someone would buy a product or service; it answers the question "What's in it for me?"

Buying signals: indications your prospect is ready to close a deal and complete the purchase

Capital purchases review: The final decision-making group or person only looks at paperwork to make an approval decision

Clarifying questions: questions that explore previous answers to expand the knowledge of the listener

C-level staff: chief executive officers, chief information officers, chief operating officers, chief financial officers, and the like

Close: making the sale

Closed-ended questions: questions that can be answered by one or two words

Closing ratio: the mathematical ratio representing the number of deals you close compared to the number of presentations you make

Cold calls: phone calls or drop-ins to attempt to get business from someone you don't know

Competitive research: Identifying your competitors and evaluating their strategies to determine their strengths and weaknesses relative to those of your own product or service

Compliant/Analytical: a person who fits the Conscientiousness profile in the DISC® profile test

Contact-management software: computer software that keeps track of all the contact information and notes for customers and prospects

Customer management or customer relationship management: practices, strategies and technologies that companies use to manage and analyze customer interactions and data throughout the customer lifecycle, with the goal of improving business relationships with customers, assisting in customer retention and driving sales

Decision maker: the person who is in charge of the money and ultimately, the decision to buy

Dialing for dollars: calling on the phone to schedule sales meetings

Direct mail: brochures, flyers, letters, etc., sent directly to a potential customer via the U.S. Postal Service or another mail or package delivery service

DISC: a personality profile test that categorizes people into Dominance (Drivers), Influencers (Expressives), Steadiness (Supportives) & Conscientiousness (Compliants/Analyticals)

Drive: an urge to attain a goal

Driver: a person who fits the Dominance personality traits found in the DISC profile test

Email marketing: direct mail that is sent via email to generate business

Features: the factual attributes of a product or service

Gatekeeper: the person in charge of keeping others and distractions from bothering the decision maker, often the receptionist, administrative assistant or purchasing agent

Goal: specific, measurable, attainable action toward a desired effect

Implication questions: questions that offer insight into why the prospect believes there is a problem

Influencer: the person who influences or impacts the decision maker to choose the purchase

Influencer/Expressive: a person who fits the Influence profile in the DISC profile test

Initiator: the person who starts the buying process, usually because of a need

IWTTIO: stands for "I want to think it over"

Kinesthetic people: people who learn by touch or feeling

Leads: unknown, unqualified sales prospects

Marketing: the activity, set of institutions, and processes for creating, communicating, delivering, and exchanging offerings that have value for customers, clients, partners, and society at large.

Modified rebuy: purchasing something that is slightly different than what was purchased previously, such as a new model of a car

Moment of magic: delivering more than the customer expects

Moment of misery: delivering less than the customer expects

Moment of truth: delivering exactly what the customer expects

Needs-payoff questions: questions that allow the customer to catalog all the benefits that will accrue when the solution is implemented

Negotiated work: a sales professional and the buying team commit to working out a solution together

New buys: purchases of items that have never been purchased previously

One-time purchases: buying an item only once

Open-ended questions: questions that require an answer that cannot be answered by one word

Pain: the reason that buyers purchase a product or service or change behavior

Personal selling: selling products and services through relationship selling

Place: distribution/location of how the product or service is delivered

Postmortem: a meeting that takes place after a sales call to evaluate the positives and negatives of the meeting

Post-sale activities: activities to set up the next sale and get referrals, including what needs to be done after the decision maker signs the contract or purchases your product to assure the sale sticks and the buyer does not renege on the purchase

Price: the monetary amount a product sells for

Probing questions: questions designed to get more details

Product: goods or services sold

Promotion: advertising, public relations (including social media, blogs and websites), customer service, sales promotions, brand awareness, direct mail, point-of-purchase displays, trade shows, sponsorships, personal selling, etc.

Prospect: someone who has a need you can meet and you wish to do business with

Public bids: vendors submit sealed proposals that are opened and read at the appointed time

Purchaser: the person who fills out the purchase paperwork, often the purchasing agent or buyer in a larger company

Qualified prospect: a potential customer that meets the buying requirements, they are the decision maker, have a solvable problem, and have the budget to solve the problem

Recurring purchases: items bought on a regular, recurring pattern

Referrals: the person or company to whom a salesperson is referred for business, often known as a "warm call" because the recipient is usually more receptive to talking with or meeting the salesperson because they know the person who referred the business

Reversal technique: the process of answering a question with a question

Reverse auction: Vendors compete electronically by putting in a bid for the project. The lowest bid amount is then shown to all bidders who have a chance to beat it

Rolodex®: a desktop card index used to record names, addresses, and telephone numbers, in the form of a rotating spindle or a small tray to which removable cards are attached

Sales: the exchange of goods, services, or property for money

Sales call: a meeting or phone conversation with a customer or potential customer

Sales cycle: the time it takes for the buyer to decide to buy a product or service

Sealed-bid purchasing: the process of buying goods through a quote or bid that is sealed when submitted to prevent other bidders from knowing the details of their bid

Specifications: the details on which to bid; specific requirements; often shortened to "specs"

SPIN selling: a method developed by Neil Rackham that helps you identify the steps of a sale. SPIN is an abbreviation for Situation, Problem, Implication, Needs Payoff

Straight rebuys: making a purchase of something that is exactly the same as purchased previously

Supportive: a person who fits the Steadiness profile in the DISC profile test

Suspect: an unqualified prospect

Testimonials: comments by previous customers that can be used to show success

Three-bid process: the process of soliciting three (or some number of) bids or quotes for the purchaser to be able to compare pricing or value-added services

Trade show: a conference or exhibition at which businesses in a particular industry promote their products and services

Treasure map: a visual representation of your goals

Unqualified prospect: a potential customer that has not been evaluated

User: the person who will be using the purchase

Visual people: people who learn primarily by seeing

BIBLIOGRAPHY

ACT! Contact Management Software, http://www.act.com/

The Four Agreements: A Practical Guide to Personal Freedom (A Toltec Wisdom Book), Don Miguel Ruis, Paperback, Amber-Allen Publishing, 1997, ISBN #1878424319

Frames of the Mind: The Theory of Multiple Intelligence, Howard Garner, Paperback, Basic Books, 1983, 2011, ISBN #978-0-465-02433-9

Influence, the Psychology of Persuasion, Revised Edition, Robert Cialdini, Paperback, William Morrow and Company, Inc., 1984, 1993, ISBN #978-0061241895

Microsoft Office Software, http://www.microsoft.com/

Purple Cow, New Edition: Transform Your Business by Being Remarkable, Seth Godin, Penguin Publishing Group, 2009, ISBN # 13: 9781591843177

The Pursuit of Happyness starring Will Smith, DVD, Screenplay by Steve Conrad, 2006

Selling the Invisible, A Field Guide to Modern Marketing, Harry Beckwith, Paperback, Time Warner Books, 1997, ISBN #0-446-52094-2

SPIN Selling, Neil Rackham, McGraw Hill, 1988, ISBN #0-07-051113-6

ABOUT THE AUTHORS

A successful salesman, sales manager and business owner, **Donald S. Crawford**, P.E., understands the selling process. His experience comes from more than 45 years of working in both large and small companies, selling technically complex products to businesses.

Lois Carter Crawford, APR, has more than 35 years of entrepreneurial experience as a business owner, writer, editor, marketing communications, and public relations professional. She works with small business owners and managers to help them with their communications needs.

ACKNOWLEDGEMENTS

Thank you to our special friends, beta readers and editors for their helpful feedback and suggestions: Mark Albright, Sandy Albright, Elizabeth Cottrell, Jennifer Cottrell, Kathleen Stinehart, and Anne Tjaden. Thank you to our patient book formatter, Emily June Street.

REVIEW THIS BOOK

Thanks for adding ***Secrets of the Softer Side of Selling*** to your library. If you liked this book and learned a tip or two, please write a review and post it on Amazon, even if it's only a few words. Potential readers rely on reviews when deciding what to purchase, and authors rely on positive reviews to sell their books. Thank you for your support!

LET'S CONNECT

We offer one-on-one and group sales training, sales coaching and mentoring, sales management training, conference and workshop presentations, and keynote speeches. We also provide marketing communications, writing and editing services for B2B companies.

We enjoy engaging with our readers. Visit our website and subscribe to our blog and email newsletter, Softer Side of Selling, and we'll give you one or more quick sales tips in every issue. Our newsletter is designed to help you attract more customers, close more sales, earn more revenue, boost your bottom line, and drive your competitors crazy. Subscribe today.

Don & Lois Crawford

www.softersideofselling.com
lois@softersideofselling.com
(540) 820-3840

www.ingramcontent.com/pod-product-compliance
Lightning Source LLC
Chambersburg PA
CBHW072223270326
41930CB00010B/1978
* 9 7 8 0 9 7 4 2 5 1 1 4 1 *